SESIL PIR

Human-Centered® Leadership
Awakening the Choice Within

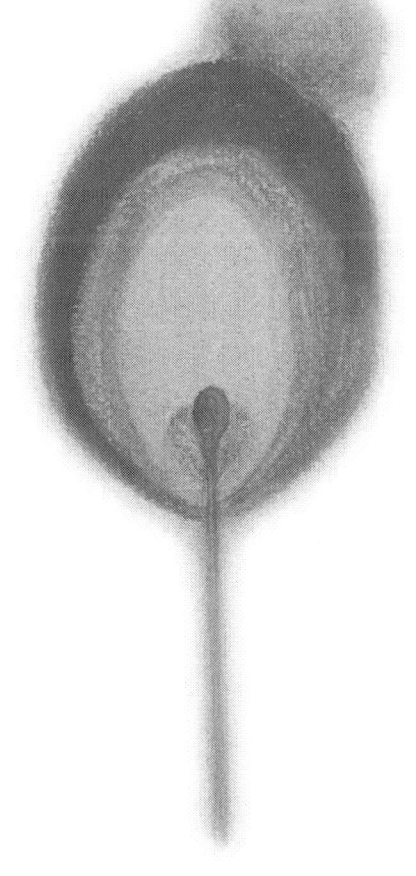

HUMAN-CENTERED LEADERSHIP
SESIL PIR

ISBN: 979-8510-499-86-5
1st Edition: May 2021

Copyrights:
© Sesil Pir
© Nefes Yayıncılık A.Ş.
Certificate No: 15747
Tuti Kitap is a Nefes Publishing brand.

All rights reserved. No parts of this publication may be reproduced in any form or by any means, electronic, mechanical, photocopying, recording or otherwise, without the prior permission of the publisher.

EDITOR: Heather Sills
COVER PAGE DESIGN: Hülya Akça
COVER ARTIST: Fateme Banishoeib
PAGE LAYOUT: Melik Uyar

TUTİ KİTAP
Bağdat Cad. No:167/2 Çatırlı Apt. B Blok D:4
Göztepe / Kadıköy / İstanbul
Phone: (216) 359 10 20 Fax: (216) 359 40 92
www.tuti.com.tr
    tutikitap@tuti.com.tr
    /tutikitap
    /tutikitap
    /tutikitap

SESIL PIR

Human-Centered™ Leadership

Awakening the Choice Within

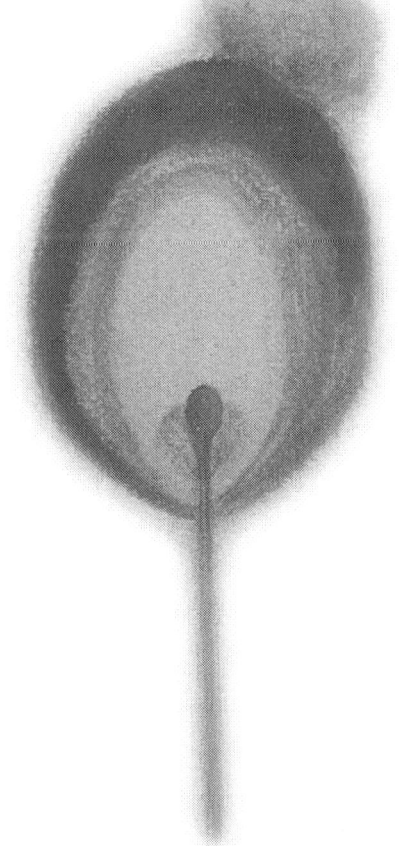

Behaviors, Mindsets, Attributes for Future of Work

tutikitap

SESİL PİR

Sesil Pir serves as Head of Employee Experience at Takeda Pharmaceuticals and CEO of SESIL PIR Consulting GmbH, a boutique management consultancy, focusing on changing the status quo of work.

Mrs. Pir is an active contributor of Forbes, has been published in the Harvard Business Review, HR Zone and UK's HR Magazine. She has contributed to many management books over the years.

She started her career as a Marketing Consultant with Deloitte & Touché in 1999. Since, she has worked for Honeywell International, Cargill Inc., Microsoft Corporation, and Novartis AG as an HR Functional Leader. She holds an MA-HRIR from Carlson School of Management, an Executive MBA from Harvard University, and a BA from Eastern Michigan University.

She has been recently recognized as '40 Thinkers Under 40' in 2017 and '101 Employee Engagement Influencers' globally in 2018, 2019, and 2020. She is married and resides in Zurich with her husband.

Contents

PREFACE 9

ACKNOWLEDGEMENTS 11

PART 1: STATUS QUO 15
The Longing 16
Hundreds of Years of Business 21
It's Business, But It's Personal Too! 28
A Broader Definition Of "Human" 33
The Higher Feeling Of Love 36
Self-Concept 40
Being 45
Relating 48
Doing 50
Reconnecting to Love 53

PART 2: BEHAVIORS & MINDSETS 59
Leadership Redefined, One Human At A Time! 60
Enabling Sustainable Growth – A Different Economical Model 68
A New Set Of Behaviors 70
A New Set Of Mindsets 77
Is It Possible To Shift A Mindset? 88

PART 3: CORE HUMAN ATTRIBUTES 91
Power of Intention 92
The Eight Core Human Attributes 95
Purpose 96
Courage 102
Foresight 108
Emotional Insight 114
Wonder 119
Wisdom 125
Compassion 131
Mastery 135

PART 4: A BEAUTIFUL WORKPLACE 145
The Soul Of An Organization 146
A Thriving Organization 147
Sense-Making 152
Culture Formation 153
Barriers To Forming Healthy Cultures 155
Accepting Change And Virtuousness 156
Beauty 157
Like A Beautiful Piece Of Art 159

Preface

For many years the success of a company was defined by share price and return on investment. Often employees were perceived as less important and, fundamentally, replaceable. There was little concern over mental health issues such as stress, anxiety, or depression and how such conditions impacted the whole workplace and ultimately the success of a company.

We now know that mental health issues have increased dramatically over the last decade and impact not only the individual but contribute to a dramatic increase in corporate expenditures not only for health care but in regard to human resources. When individuals are suffering this also results in a lack of engagement, lower productivity, and decreased creativity.

Over the last decade, new findings in neuroscience and organizational psychology have given us incredible insights into the concept of human thriving and its impact on the work environment. Fundamentally, humans thrive when they are respected, given dignity, listened to, and feel psychologically safe. It is in this environment that engagement, creativity, and productivity dramatically increase.

In this engaging and thought-provoking book, the author, Sesil Pir, uses these findings to outline a path to create compassionate and heart-centered organizations. To some who read these words, this may seem foreign, "soft" or not necessary, but there is an ever increasing body of evidence that when companies create an environment centered on human thriving, everyone benefits: the company, the leadership, and the employees. It is instilling such values that truly defines a "successful" company.

James R. Doty, M.D.

Founder & Director of the Stanford University Center for Compassion and Altruism Research and Education

Senior Editor of the Oxford Handbook of Compassion Science

New York Times bestselling author of Into the Magic Shop: A Neurosurgeon's Quest to Discover the Mysteries of the Brain and the Secrets of the Heart

Acknowledgements

For the first time at 39, I feel I have come to discover the true meaning of my name.

Cecile, the origin of my name, a rare flower that blossoms thru the solid rock, mostly found in the higher altitudes. A few weeks ago, sitting by the Indian Ocean on a small, reserved island and holding a beautiful book by Mark Nepo, I was reflecting on how in Japan, one of my most favorite geographies and cultures in the world, there is an art form called 'kintsugi'. This is an art of filling cracks with gold. Then, all of a sudden it occured to me that it is not filling, rather entering the cracks, embracing the space that reveals the gold. We carry what matters inside all along. It is our years of experience that waters the unique seed, giving it strength to come out of the dark. Sun radiates onto its shades until finally, the soul sprouts through the cracks from unknown into the known world. That, I realized, may be just what is *becoming...*

Human-centered leadership is born out of an awakening of that seed, fed by many years of helpless, horrifying, anxious experiences. I have come to believe those who haven't witnessed self-transform into an ill-tempered child by the chase of ego and often in the name of love haven't really transcended in their unique stories. Though deeply wired for connection and purpose, humans tend to hide under comfortable circumstances, mostly floating along the surface. It is only when the world grows unsafe or life presents us with stresses that bring forth feelings of self-doubt, worry, sorrow, our devotion to the path is tested. Paradoxically, it is in those moments of loss, uncertainty, or sadness we calibrate and discover our capacity for who we are. Then, our choice leads us into an intuited practice.

I hope you'd consider it fair for me to say the recent pandemic experience has made the separation between the self and the other, the individual and the collective, the system and the leader even more clear to the eye and has highlighted the many ways in which we have come to undermine our individual powers and shrink collective capacities. From East to West, we all seek better collaboration and higher cooperation across borders. We all ache for organizations that drive value beyond profit. We all search for communities that offer equal opportunity of belonging and be guided by leaders that offer safe, grounded, and joyful connections.

This book is a testimony to a shared belief across many communities and geographies that redefining leadership, enabling the evolution of current organizational models, and debating conventional mindsets can slowly help shift cultures inside workplaces. It is also a humble invitation to a journey of self-discovery in activating inner powers, exercising better choice and being mindful of the climate impact we generate inside our workplaces.

I hope taking a formal stand in a regenerative process towards re-envisioning realities will have a ripple effect into the future and support sustainable development of our societies that offer better equity, equality, and dignity for the humankind.

I am incredibly thankful for Dr. James Doty, who has opened the doors of Stanford University and the Center for Compassion, Altruism Research, and Education (CCARE) for our collaborative study. I am incredibly thankful for Dr. Sinan Canan, who has brainstormed around the core human attributes pulling from ancient wisdom and Anatolian values. I am incredibly thankful for my mentors Carol Bubar, Dr. Jonathan Younger, Dr. John Budd and for my spiritual guides, my maternal grandmother, Dr. Cemalnur Sargut and Dr. Susan Cain, who have consciously and unconsciously pulled up mirrors for me to self-reflect upon over the many years. I am incredibly thankful for Hulya Akca, who leads our creative story, for my publisher and friend, Kerim Guc, who believes in me becoming a vehicle of service. I am thankful for my colleagues, Dr. Monica Worline and Asli Aker's dedication to our research and content development processes; and for Fateme Banishoeb, both for her partnership to the journey and for gifting us with the gentlest cover drawing. Finally, I am incredibly thankful for my friends, colleagues, who inspire me every day and for my family, who have surely become a witness to my journey.

This book is dedicated to my angel dad, who left this world way too early.

When everything is falling apart, it means something new is emerging...

With gratitude,

Sesil Pir
Zurich, April 2021

PART 1

STATUS QUO

It had been four years and a few months since I had been hired into my corporate executive position.

During our initial discussions, I understood the organization was on the cusp of a portfolio shift and there was a desire for transformation. I had spoken with 15 stakeholders over two days – 6 HR professionals, 6 business leaders, and 3 additional people I would never get to meet or work with during my entire tenure at the company. Looking back, this was a sign of lack of ownership in decision making. For every value-related question I posed, I received a different answer from different stakeholders. I didn't think too much of it at the time, but this was a sign of lack of value alignment. During my conversation with the CHRO, she announced to me how she had made two people's lives "miserable" because "they have eventually become uncontrollable". Once again, I overlooked the severity of the warning signs.

The truth is that my desire to land another top corporate position with a remuneration package to match was overpowering my ability to face reality. The fear of missing out on an opportunity had paralyzed my ability to think clearly, and the appeal of holding a head of department role had paralyzed my ability to analyze the situation objectively. So, I made an emotional decision and accepted the offer even though my heart had doubts about the people and the company culture.

After hours of hard work, sweat, tears, and endlessly going into "battle" for our people, I came out the other side with some savings, two rashes, an uncontrollable thyroid, and a very fragile relationship.

After four years of commitment and devotion, I woke up one morning and handed in my resignation. No second thoughts.

THE LONGING

Work serves as a source of many things for the leaders of today: Economic gain, social status, a sense of identity. Even though there is considerable research into the impact of work on our lives, we, as modern world leaders, tend to pay more attention to profitability. This is primarily because our current working practices were developed by industrialists and modern economists who put profit-making at the core. This means we often use salary to rationalize decision making.

Looking back over my time in Paris, I now clearly see that I, too, had willingly fallen into the same trap as many of us frequently fall into. The story goes like this: The more you work, the more you get rewarded with a broader scope and a prestigious title. The more you are able to get results through that broader scope, the more you get rewarded in compensation. The more you get rewarded in compensation, the more you self-identify with the company brand. It sounds like a cycle of addiction. And, in fact, it is. Research has shown us that the brain scans of people who are about to make money look very much like the brain scans of those on cocaine.

Is being "high" only something a few people experience? Certainly not…

It is no secret that while 21st-century businesses hustle to adapt and organizations compete fiercely for agility, a significant portion of our global workforce struggles to find their sense of belonging. For some, this new era of unlimited possibilities has ushered in prosperity and the potential to address some of humanity's most vexing challenges in creative new ways. For others, the constant technological and social change continuously triggers isolation, loneliness, and fear. This is the paradox of our current situation. While we are now in a better position to end poverty, cure disease, and create wealth than ever before in human history, global engagement surveys across the board report that our workforce is feeling disengaged, distracted, and unappreciated.

As an industrial and organizational psychologist, a practitioner, and just someone curious about the human condition, I find it appalling to read through some of the latest workplace statistics.

Let's take a closer look at four examples:

> "44% of people leaders (executives and managers combined) believe their company is adequately prepared for digitalization."
>
> MIT Sloan Management Review, in collaboration with Deloitte.

I find this an interesting statistic because it suggests that, although we read and talk about strategizing for the future of work, it seems we are yet to take any action to actually prepare for it. This lack of readiness, or resistance to sustainable business transformation, is likely an outcome of a variety of factors. In some cases, it could be related to not understanding or internalizing the context at large; in others, it may be related to not having enough resources or appetite for change. Or it could simply point to the comfort of the status quo. Whatever the underlying reasons, it does not change the fact that the global workforce will continue to be stretched to try and meet the demands of both the "old" and the "new" world order. This will likely result in continued and perhaps increased tension, exhaustion, and stress.

> "Only 26% of human resource departments and 38% of leaders reported that the current quality of the leadership in their organizations could be rated as "excellent" or "very good"."
>
> DDI's Global Leadership Forecast (GLF)

The way I interpret this statistic is that, at best, ~60% of our people leaders are not considered "high quality" by their peers or human resources practitioners. In response, I can't help but ask: Given the number of ivy league schools specializing in business administration and management, and preparing the next generation of leaders; given we view these institutions as top caliber and turn to their researchers for vision, trendsetting, and talent pools, how in the world are we facing such a big skills gap? We would not consider anyone with less than excellent references for a childcare role, so why do we think it is okay to entrust our adult experiences to those who are not equipped to fulfill the role? Which knowledge, mindset, and skills are our educational institutions actually equipping our future leaders with? What is the impact of having low-caliber leaders shape our unique experiences day to day? And, most importantly, how is this affecting our collective progress?

> "69% of managers are uncomfortable communicating with employees."
> Quartz at Work

Another breathtaking statistic: If the whole idea of hierarchy in business is to get results through the leadership of others, how is it possible that almost 70% of our leaders are not comfortable communicating with us? What is it that makes our leaders feel uncomfortable? What is getting in the way of their effective behavior modeling? And if they do not have the required skills or courage, how are they managing to communicate with their employees?

> "80% of students value achievement over kindness."
> KQED MindShift

This last statistic I find the most concerning. There is so much embedded in this short statement that I am not sure where to begin, except to ask: What are the specific definitions of success, underlying messages, and overt behaviors we are actively role modeling for our kids and generations to come? What is making them think that achieving a goal will be more fulfilling than caring for others?

There is a deep and silent suffering inside our organizations. Sometimes this manifests itself in mental health problems such as sadness, anxiety, depression or sleep disorders; sometimes in cardiac defects in the form of heart attacks, sudden cardiac death, hypertension or strokes; or in mind/body disconnects like headaches or gastrointestinal disorders such as constipation, irritable bowel syndrome, hemorrhoids, and anal fissures, among others.

We have people sitting quietly at their desks pretending to get by while, deep inside, they are longing for joy and aching for connection. We have people working overtime to make ends meet while consistently being undervalued. We have people who are physically present, but who at the same time feel totally disconnected from their true sense of being. We have people who are aware of the pain, yet do not know how to break the cycle, only to let apathy trap them further still.

We must recognize that these human conditions are very hard to detect from the outside and even harder to express from the inside. This intangibility is precisely the reason we need to acknowledge that our work-experience story is facing a crisis of confidence. The growing distance between production and consumption, the commercial and domestic, leadership and followership, coupled with the demands of our modern lives, makes a big portion of our workforce feel overly activated, alienated, increasingly anxious, and sad. The dissatisfaction, discrimination, and harassment we turn the other cheek to is robbing people of their right to dignity, equity, and equality.

We may be starting to understand the tension future change drivers bring into the workplace. Yet, we still do not understand that the developments we are observing create not only a need for advanced organizational interventions, but also a space for mental freedom and imagination, new demands for our inner sources in search of more holistic experiences. This is the essence of Alena Chapman's book *You Can't Escape from a Prison if You Don't Know You're in One.*

We, as a species, are not quite equipped to deal with the competing priorities, increasing complexities, and ever-changing dynamics of our modern lives. Until we acknowledge the pain we are collectively in, accept our individual role in the creation of that reality, and visualize an evolutionary future that will bring us more meaning, we will remain a prisoner to our circumstances – both inside and outside the workplace.

It is time we blow up the myth that our way of being – physically, mentally, spiritually and emotionally – does not matter at work. What future organizations need is not only workspaces that look fun and differentiated benefits packages, but also specific human-centered goals that aim to bring our employees fulfillment each and every day. We need a desire to create a differentiated approach, a new economic model and a value-based environment that can help individuals thrive and strive towards a new level of collective potential.

This book, then, intends to serve both as a manifesto, giving voice to all those suffering in silence, and a spiritual guide for aspiring leaders of the 21st century. It intends to acknowledge the loss of collective productivity and the search for meaning. It invites businesses to take a more humanistic view when they build their stories, and to develop creative organizational practices that can activate a new kind of thriving. Most importantly, it aims to engage the next-generation leaders in a regenerative process to shape the future into the kind of trust-based, compassionate work environments we all long to become a part of.

There is a call to expand our capacities at work. That capacity growth requires us to become resilient, exercise more consciousness, and take accountability in the process of rebuilding as independent agents. The future of work is about individual transcendence to enable a broader culture transformation. This is not just a call for those at the top, either; it is for every level of our enterprises. Each one of us is being asked to know who we are, to connect multitudes of our "being", and practice self-leadership, before we "relate" with others and entertain new ways of "doing".

Remember that copying the status quo is easy; pretending to rebuild it is even easier.

It is time we acknowledge that working harder, longer, and faster to innovate from the outside is a dream we never realized. Creating a new paradigm of work is the real innovation we desire. There is no shortage of good ideas, good products or good pieces of the pie. There will always be new markets and opportunities. But right now, in this unique period of transition, what we really need is to seek to build good lives, something which is truly and rapidly becoming harder to come by.

HUNDREDS OF YEARS OF BUSINESS

Humanity is going through an unprecedented transformation.

The impact of the Fourth Industrial Revolution is like something we have never seen before. The forces of globalization, digitalization, and democratization are shifting the way we work and live our lives big time. While smart technologies, robots, and artificial intelligence continue to impact our day-to-day choices and life experiences, increasingly we find ourselves having a harder time envisioning the future. Did you know that 52% of all Fortune 500 companies have completely disappeared since the year 2000? How about the fact that the average lifecycle of an organization nose-dived from 75 years in 1955 to 15 years in 1975? We also have no idea what that number will be in the next 10 years.

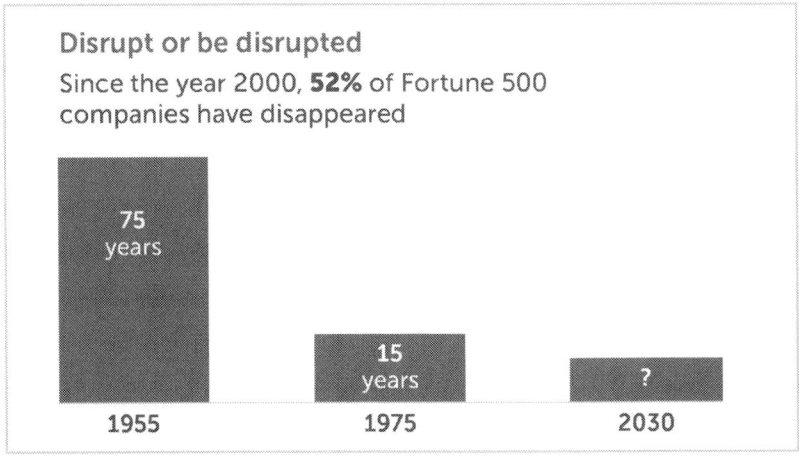

Table 1. Longevity of Disruption

The truth is that today's organizations were never designed to evolve proactively and sustainably. Instead, they were built for just-in-time discipline and efficiency, enforced through hierarchy and routinization, resulting in often short-term gains. As society shifts, a mismatch has developed between the pace of change in the way we lead our lives, and the speed of change at which most organizations can respond. The way we define, organize, and manage work as a result of previous industrial revolutions is no longer serving our integrated life needs. More importantly, the archaic methodologies and technologies we continue to leverage inside our organizations cause more stress, anxiety, and isolation for our people inside our workplaces.

When we look at the history of business, it is inarguable that extraordinary developments have taken place in our global economies over the last two hundred years. We have experienced a steady and progressive shift from manufacturing to information societies, and witnessed the transition from physical labor to mental work. Without a doubt, we have benefited greatly from the previous industrial revolutions. But we could also argue that there has been such major development of business processes that to many the concept of "work" has become an overwhelmingly complex and cumbersome experience. While work processes have become blueprinted, employees struggle to find the white space they need for creativity. While research and development cycles have become better regulated, people have come to find that the level of granularity and validation sometimes makes innovation impossible. While manufacturing lines have expanded from one part of the world to another, people have come to face more challenges in effective communication and connectivity. While organizations are now structured by units and matrices to better handle their enlarged scope and need to scale, people have become unsure of their boundaries for accountability. There is an incredible amount of organizational complexity built into our everyday practices, and evidently it has made our lives significantly more difficult to manage in places.

Because of this dichotomy, it is important to step back and remind ourselves that human beings did not always live or work in the way we do today. World economies did not exist until very recently. Our current economic modeling and the way we have come to view and engage in business is the result of an evolution.

If we look at the history of labor, for example, we find that selling time in exchange for money is actually a relatively new idea. This does not mean that for years we were sitting around doing nothing. On the contrary. As human beings, we were constantly engaged in one life-giving activity or another. We searched and collected food for our families, we kept ourselves busy by wood carving, painting, and making tools, etc. Way before town or country economies took over, we had simple household economies – initially hunting animals, later growing crops and, after the domestication of animals, engaging in trade. Over time and in response to the increased desires and curiosities of our families, we slowly started exchanging goods on an ever-increasing scale, which led to the creation of a barter system.

Money was only introduced as a later step, and as a way of solving many problems created by the barter system. So, human beings have always been curious animals. During this exchange of goods and services, some found themselves wondering if *their* share of goods or services was worth more than that of their neighbors. Money solved that kind of curiosity. But it also did something else. It opened the door to specialization of labor and unionization of work groups. Once we discovered there was more money to be made, we started looking for new ways to expand. As our economies grew reliably, we settled down in fixed geographies, turning these communal spaces into commercial town centers. From there, it was not long before national and eventually global economies developed. Here, we experienced large-scale production and distinguished services, widening the market to an unprecedented, international level.

It is important we recognize that other socio-cultural developments took place alongside this economic progress. While at the beginning our economies were mainly shared, when labor became specialized and markets expanded, our economic and social worlds started to split off from one another. Back in the "good old days", we used to know exactly where the apple we had for breakfast came from. But over time we became accustomed to not knowing where our food and other produce comes from. Today, a large majority of us have no idea who makes the clothes we wear or the chairs we sit on, let alone the food we eat day to day. The advancement of our economies has created more distance between us and our neighbors, our goods and their providers, our immediate communities and larger societies.

This economic development also triggered new labor models. Once upon a time, there were no dotted-line or matrix models, so we had to redesign our production models to respond to our growing business needs. This introduced another interesting pattern we have been observing in the last several hundred years – the evolution of production.

In the late 1800s and early 1900s, the main focus of our businesses was on production. Our biggest concern was about getting a new product onto the market. This is why the period from the American Civil War until about the 1920s would eventually become known as the "Mass Production Era". Following the First Industrial Revolution, the agricultural and colonial business models that had slowly dominated the world for centuries gave way to the development of production. From the end of the 19st century into the 1930s, limited industrial supply meant that producing goods guaranteed almost consistent sales. People not only needed goods; they *wanted* to own stuff to advance the quality of their lives. Advances in production machinery allowed businesses to produce more, so it is no surprise then that manufacturing models became extremely popular. More production meant more sales and production models relied on machinery to achieve the necessary economies of scale, often pushing costs lower and increasing overall profits. Some economists, like Thomas S. Ashton or Friedrich A. Hayek, even go so far as to say that the biggest impact the First Industrial Revolution had was that the standard of living for the Western world's general population began to steadily increase for the first time in history. Whether that is true or not, the First Industrial Revolution definitely marked a major turning point in the evolution of business and human history. As a result, almost every aspect of daily life was influenced in some way.

By the 20th century, the first era of globalization had begun[1]. When the 1950s came along, our focus switched from purely production to offering products and services at the same time. Industrialization allowed cheaper production of household items, and while industrial supply increased, it also had a disruptive impact on the market. Many companies began to face tougher competition. With the introduction of the "Marketing Era", businesses learned that they needed to set themselves apart in the marketplace if they wanted to gain competitive advantage. Business models began to shift toward market segmentation and developing unique ways to differentiate brands. Marketing campaigns became just as important as manufacturing capacity. Market research became the starting point for product-development efforts. Those that could better differentiate themselves started to be seen as more successful or powerful, which led to a widening separation from those that could not. This resulted in the more successful brands acting in ways that only benefited their own position rather than collective behavior for the good of the whole market. In the end, brand pricing efforts arose as a new driver of business profitability and differentiation started to service the sharpening of the capitalistic view.

As globalization gained momentum and businesses became increasingly efficient in marketing and brand differentiation, savvy entrepreneurs began to realize long-term customer relationships and brand champions might be the key to survival as we entered the 21st century. In this expanded world order, businesses could now serve customers in a much larger area, and more open and efficient communication was also possible. During this period, which will later be referred to as the "Customer Era", solutions rather than products or brand pricing became the new paradigm.

Today, the world of business is all anchored to relatedness. Since the 1990s, the current "Relationship Era" has mixed elements of each previous era and workforce planning while offering the experiences of the future powered by some of the most rapid technological development we have seen since the First Industrial Revolution. Firstly, companies

---

[1]   https://www.wikiwand.com/en/History_of_capitalism

can connect with global customers in more direct and meaningful ways than ever before – thanks to the advancement of the internet and supporting platforms. Secondly, crowdsourcing has altered development models to seek product-input or start-up capital directly from consumers through a two-way conversation. As a result, brand positioning and utilization strategies have become more targeted. While lean models gained increasing popularity amid a focus on core competency gain, the use of contractors for specialized functions has increased.

Now, that was several hundred years of history in a mere nutshell but it still begs the question of how we have managed to scale this fast and whether we have done so effectively.

We were certainly considerably quick to learn how to organize and govern at scale. We discovered, for example, that to reach a certain level of efficiency, it may make sense to bring people under one roof and structure and monitor through hierarchies. Today, we have three primary strategies for organizing and governing our work: centralized, decentralized, and distributed[2] (also referred to as traditional, strategic, and transformative.) Roughly 50% of our global organizations sit in the strategic space when it comes to division and delegation of workload, and we know more and more are wanting to evolve into the transformative space[3].

Another efficiency measure we discovered was routinization. The automation of routine tasks was introduced to be able to control the rate of production and quality assurance. Over the years, though, evidence has shown that routinization has contributed to the polarization of labor markets. Labor market polarization is the phenomenon of rising wages and higher employment of both high- and low-skill labor relative to those in the middle[4], which has come to be known as the "hollowing out" of the middle. Through routinization, the routine tasks that middle-skilled workers used to perform can be easily

---

2   https://journals.sagepub.com/doi/full/10.1177/2631787720977052
3   https://journals.sagepub.com/doi/full/10.1177/2631787720977052
4   Autor, Katz and Kearney 2006; Goos and Manning 2007; Autor and Dorn 2013; Goos, Manning and Salomon 2014; Beaudry, Green and Sand 2016

automated, by information and computer technologies, which over time has led to an increase in job losses and weak wage growth as the price of computer capital rapidly[5] declined.

Why does it matter how we came to scale, you might ask? It matters because when we put the technological examples that helped us scale on the table at once, we find many of them have been developed, and if not, highly influenced, by the industrialists of their time. Industrialists, by definition, are the most influential in leading businesses, and are mostly profit-focused. They are industry creators, often most interested and invested in maximizing productivity to extract the largest amount of profit. This is not to say they are evil people. On the contrary, much of the current economic set-up and societal wealth we benefit from is a byproduct of the industrialists' influence. We must be clear, however, that industrialists are rarely interested in creativity or change. Their interests lie in protecting the existing status quo. And this is where a potential issue arises. Though industrialists may be fundamental for the existence of today's economic, industrial and socio-cultural modeling, many are not really interested in offering hope or promise for a different kind of reality. Therefore, considering the current change in the broader landscape, and assuming there is no change in the industrialists' main philosophies on the horizon, we will continue to see a growing gap between the expectations of the industrialists and the workers who are vital for their success.

This is why we must acknowledge that there are other more scientific and human-focused ways to create value. The kind of demand-based view is no longer helping our organizations differentiate. The description we proudly used for business over the years has been "money-making machine". Similarly, the mantra we proudly carried inside our human resources departments has been "having the right people, in the right place, at the right time." Unfortunately, neither of these views is enough to create the kind of platform that would support the amount of variability, ambiguity, and change we see in the current environment, nor can it satisfy the dreams of our future consumers.

---

5   Acemoglu and Autor 2011

IT'S BUSINESS, BUT IT'S PERSONAL TOO!

Change is the only constant in this new era. The question is no longer about whether we should try to direct the forces of change, but rather about whether we are ready to accept that change is a given, and shift our status quo, our ways of working, to adjust to this new norm. The ideals of efficiency and control, the two most common concepts of management, were derived directly from Newtonian physics. We can replace these with today's importance of information, but these are all just terms. Instead, we need to focus on changing the behavior. What we need to recognize is that we are now in the "Experience Era", and what we need is not more information, rather wisdom that requires human experience and compassion inside our workplaces.

This is indeed a cultural change and one that needs a brand-new philosophy compared to industrial development. It shines a light on a number of difficulties facing us inside of our organizations. Let's take a look at some statistics below:

Workplace statistics

~48%	~32%	~10%
of people feeling 'unsatisfied' at work CONFERENCE BOARD	of US workers are engaged vs. ~13% of global workforce GALLUP	are concerned about an individual at work they fear could become violent AMERICAN WORKPLACE
~40%	**~10%**	**4x**
of workers reported their job was very or extremely stressful NIOSH	of the world's population lives on less than $2 per day WORLD BANK	Young workers job insecurity or unemployment compared to elders WORLD BANK
9,5 million People in the United States work full time and still fall under the poverty line US BUREAU OF LABOR STATISTICS		Gender pay gap is to close by **2186** WEF

Table 2. Workplace Statistics at a Glance

These are only a handful of statistics that merely scratch the surface of the *silent suffering* experienced by our most important asset – people across our global workforce.

According to the World Health Organization (WHO), depression, which is already the leading cause of long-term illness, is going to be the leading global health epidemic by 2030. The primary reason for depression is reported to be work-related stress. Around the world today, we have 320 million people living with depression, and the number has increased by a drastic 18% between 2005 and 2015. There is a genuine search for meaning, inspiration, safety, and joy inside our workplaces.

In the US alone, the cost of depression for businesses is estimated to be anywhere between 2 and 3 billion USD annually. That's billions, not millions! Imagine what could be done with that sort of money to help our social communities in need. It is tragic that while some of us are exploring going to the moon or building robot dogs to detect your foot odor levels, there are many genuinely struggling to simply find their place in the world.

Furthermore, the evidence shows that, just like our businesses, our evolutionary human bodies were never built to respond to today's hectic, non-stop environments. After all, we are still operating with our primate brain and response systems[6]. This is why, during times of fear, we revert back to our basic autonomous systems.

It should not come as a surprise then that despite the vast amount of technological investments organizations have been making over the last 50 years, according to the OECD (Organisation for Economic Co-operation and Development), most countries' GDP productivity growth is tumbling downwards[7].

The latest Compendium of Productivity Indicators suggests the trend has intensified the impact of weak business investment on productiv-

---

6   https://www.ncbi.nlm.nih.gov/pmc/articles/PMC2409100/
7   https://www.oecd.org/sdd/productivity-stats/continued-slowdown-in-productivity-growth-weighs-down-on-living-standards.htm

Table 3. OECD Productivity Levels

ity growth. According to the report, the downward pressure on wages may have allowed firms to defer investment decisions, and instead meet increasing demand by hiring additional staff and, in turn, undermining the potential for investment. The OECD says productivity is ultimately a question of "working smarter" – measured by "multifactor productivity" – rather than "working harder". This view reflects an organization's ability to produce more output by better combining inputs through new ideas, technological innovations, as well as by way of process and organizational innovations. Yet it completely overlooks the fact that, aside from capability, business needs people to function properly. Organizations are living organisms, human activity systems, and their capacity can be shrunk or enlarged by circumstances. This is because living organisms are capable of self-maintenance, self-renewal, and self-transcendence[8] (Capra, 1996).

The argument that the main purpose of business is, well, business is a fundamental misconception. This core belief continues to be the feeder in the "fight" for market domination and profitability. But it is also the primary cause of the suffering we witness inside our systems.

---

[8]   https://connect.springerpub.com/content/book/978-0-8261-9552-4/part/part02/chapter/ch06

This belief suggests there is an evolutionary cause to our individual and collective existence, and it cannot be influenced. In reality, however, evolution is a process of self-organization – from an individual entity to complex networks and systems. It is no longer "business as usual"; however, for business to adopt a long-term view, there has to be a true understanding, grounded in evolutionary systems theory, open to new possibilities for redefining leadership and culture toward sustainability.

Evolution, in terms of a common definition, is often seen as a process of "survival of the fittest", implying that there may be a clever selection process. To outsmart it, egoism and selfishness are genetically embedded in our DNA. This is one of the biggest – if not *the* biggest – dogmas of current Western societies. We are made to believe that there is just not enough to go around, and everyone, without exception, is out to get the biggest piece of the pie they can. As a result, everything we set up in our societies – from primary education to institutionalized health care to global business models – is rooted in a focus on scarcity.

In schools, we ask our children to study harder and outdo their classmates on a test. In the workplace, we calibrate our employees' contribution in ranking. At home, we evaluate a neighbors' worth by how expensive their car or garden furniture is. Krista Tippett put it beautifully in her book *Becoming Wise*, "In our lives, every vision must begin and end in an economic argument in order to be heard." We are taught and reinforced to believe that, for any act to be meaningful, it has to bring about profit. We measure impact and significance through volume, and wonder why we are suffering in the process. The truth is that the number of patients or clinics is not witness to how well we cure or offer comfort to the sick and elderly. The scale of protocol or technology does not guarantee efficiency. Being busy does not always equate to productivity. In an evolutionary context, there is and must be a constant craving for rediscovery.

The term "survival of the fittest" is often attributed to Charles Darwin, yet, it was actually coined by Herbert Spencer and the Social

Darwinists, who wished to justify class and race superiority. Darwin's message was, however, quite to the contrary. He argued that evolutionary success was more dependent on fellow feeling than exclusive self-interest. He writes in chapter four of his book *On Sociability*, "Communities which included the greatest number of the most sympathetic members would flourish best, and rear the greatest number of offspring." Contrary to common belief, Darwin rather argued that there is interconnectedness to being. He understood that contemporary societies and business are inseparable. As we, human beings, are dependent on the planet, today's organizations have to collaborate within the ecosystem. From a systems perspective, we need to be fed and feed one another – individuals, institutions, the environment. We cannot detach the economy from society or the natural environment. Only an integrated approach can bring about a renewed vision for sustainability[9] (Milbrath 1989, p. 82).

Yet, again, this understanding has hardly been reflected in the way our business communities function. As the American poet and cultural critic Wayne Koestenbaum (in his essay "Labarre", 2000) points out, "an evolutionary transformation of who we are, how we behave, how we think, and what we value" is necessary to resolve the paradox between the way we operate our businesses and the collective global challenges that call for our social and environmental responsibility.

There is more to our being as living species than self-interest. We have an intrinsic need to care, to connect and to participate in meaningful life experiences as an evolutionary species[10]. As human beings, we are on a quest for purpose, meaning, and fulfillment, which has been left behind for centuries. When it comes to the creation of our human experiences and realization of our identities, we have a number of intrinsic and extrinsic motives that serve us[11]. We understand that the social and cultural factors we form facilitate and at times largely

---

9   https://www.researchgate.net/publication/228368126_The_Evolution_of_Business_Learning_innovation_and_sustainability_in_the_21_st_century

10 https://www.ncbi.nlm.nih.gov/pmc/articles/PMC2864937/

11 https://www.ncbi.nlm.nih.gov/pmc/articles/PMC2864937/

affect our sense of volition and initiative. We grasp the magnitude of conditions and their impact to hinder or elevate the quality of our capabilities and capacities.

For organizations to evolve into sustained growth models, there has to be an increased understanding of the human condition – what makes individuals thrive on their way to productivity, as well as a deepened understanding of the conditions necessary to create a flourishing culture. Businesses are uniquely positioned to shift from volume-based metrics to value-based measures and reconnect to their core purpose of serving humanity. Unfortunately, many feel that the idea of human-centeredness, or the call to focus on humanity, is just a catchphrase. Some interpret it as caring only about the human beings, others understand it as making employees key stakeholders, others believe it is – yet another – humanitarian movement raised by a few disgruntled employees.

A BROADER DEFINITION OF "HUMAN"

Though employees remain undoubtedly a primary stakeholder for future organizations, and though we see a need for organizations to make them a key priority, we need to highlight the fact that the term "human" goes way beyond a human being in its current philosophy.

In its most common usage, the word "human" generally refers to the only still-existing species of the genus Homo – anatomically and behaviorally describing modern Homo sapiens sapiens as we know it.

In scientific terms, the meaning of "human" has changed on several occasions, pointing to a diverse group of animalistic species over time. In anthropology, some identify the category of the human with the species Homo sapiens; others equate it to the whole genus Homo. Some restrict it to the subspecies Homo sapiens sapiens, while a few others take it to encompass the entire hominin lineage. Finally, in the discipline of psychology, humans designate a certain taxonomic category in which having a physiology is not sufficient to belong to the category. Although the concept of a human vastly varies in definition etymologically speaking, philosophers distinguish the linguistic meaning of indexical expressions from their content. As such, the content of an indexical is whatever it names.

Another example comes from a collaborative study between the University of Washington and Osaka University, professors Kahn et al., where scholars tried to characterize what it means to be human[12] to aid robotics design and interactions. They were able to name 10 different aspects to being human, ranging from practicing autonomy to engagement in creativity to carrying moral value and caring about reciprocity.

The descriptions are relevant because they each provide different angles on the way we define something.

What we are witnessing in the way we have and continue to define a human is that humanness is, and continues to be, a direction. If we were to write a poem about it, it would likely read something like this: "With every step I do, I walk to you, because who am I and who are you without each other?" In other words, there is a constant across many definitions that suggests there is a relational aspect to humanness.

According to the Oxford English Dictionary, the "hu" of human represents the soul of any being – physical and other dimensional as a representative part of a bigger creation. It suggests that any being with a soul, living and nonliving, may exist but cannot thrive and reach its potential without the other/the opposite. With that in mind, when we point to the growing need to focus on humanity as the centerpiece of our 21st-century organizations, we are referring to human beings (you and me alike) as a key part. But we are also referring to the natural environment and the natural life cycle of other beings, without which we cannot survive, and the robotics and intelligent machinery we will have to rely on in the future.

The business world is heavily influenced by images and metaphors that shape the strategies, structures, and processes of our organiza-

---

12   https://depts.washington.edu/hints/publications/407_kahn.pdf

tions. Therefore, taxonomy is a critical first step to creating unprecedented experiences, as that language will then shape our way of becoming, relating, and doing/working through philosophy. Once our taxonomy is enlarged, however, we must establish new bearings. We cannot evaluate the trajectory of our businesses separate from civilization and without a clear appreciation of an enlarged definition of humanity. Just as we cannot separate technology from new world order or 21st-century business, a business cannot single-handedly be oriented toward profit-making if they want to survive history. Business is not and cannot be a thing in itself, isolated from economics, society or culture.

That centering on humanness brings relativity with a potential to drive equality and dignity into the conversation that is otherwise missing. That centering gives us the benefit to claim that every time we single out our focus, such as by going after only profit or when we categorize each other, we are breaking down multiplicities and removing neutrality to offer equitable choices. Realize that when we are not actively working towards unity under a set of agreed-upon values that honor everyone equally, we are, indeed, dis-serving our initial intent and becoming blind-sided to possibilities.

Research[13] validates that high-performing organizations carry spirituality, and that they have a much deeper connection and better self-righting mechanisms than their peers. The individual employees inside organizations where we record sustained growth over time often demonstrate greater self-mastery and higher self-respect, which allows them to operate on a basis of trust, creativity, and collaboration. They take full accountability for dealing with and resolving issues, even if doing so introduces more emotional risk for them individually. Ultimately, these organizations see every single challenge as a collective opportunity.

Once again, it is those businesses that act like living organisms that will become a kind of learning organization, observing the reality

---

13 https://www.researchgate.net/publication/46175499_Spirituality_and_Performance_in_Organizations_A_Literature_Review

they create and reacting to the information in the system in a replenishing way. As paradoxical as it may seem, the success of businesses hoping to take advantage of this new revolution depends on their capacity to put humanity at the center. For our work experiences to be reinvented, we must reflect on new ways of understanding and fulfilling people's needs, a new economic model that can see beyond profit, and a new social contract that can bring it altogether.

Ultimately, workplace transformations[14] are no longer something for the distant future. Where traditional value chains are being collapsed and new market innovations are being sought out by the minute, we invite business and its leaders to engage in a regenerative process. And to take advantage of a rapidly closing window in which to create the future of work, providing the generations that follow with dignified, equal and equitable experiences.

THE HIGHER FEELING OF LOVE

I remember the first time I was knowingly cruel towards someone. It must have been when I was around eleven or twelve years old because it was during a summer before I lost my father in a traffic accident at the age of thirteen.

I grew up in the beautiful, historic city of Istanbul. My parents were products of two very different families and were both largely discriminated against for marrying outside of their clan. As a result, we were on the edge of poverty throughout my childhood, and I ended up living with my maternal grandparents from the age of two roughly until I was about nine.

My grandparents lived in the neighborhood of Balat, which is considered the "old city" of Istanbul along the Golden Horn. Our flat was the smallest of all the apartments in the building and we originally had our bathrooms outside. My grandfather slept in one room and the other room was for my grandmother, myself, and two uncles. My grandparents were

---

[14] https://whirlingchief.com/wp-content/uploads/2019/11/Human-Centered-Organizations-eGuide_181119-1.pdf

farmers. They grew corn and sold it at the "bazaar", the open market locals shopped at twice a week. By the time I was six, I was considered capable enough to help out with family chores and I was proud to do so. When not in school, I worked alongside my grandpa in the market, selling glasses of water to contribute to the family income.

We were poor. I remember noticing my grandmother budgeting for food. Once when I wanted to buy a piece of chocolate at the market, she knelt down and said "You always assume we have enough to buy but we don't this week, my sweetheart. It would be nice to ask if we have enough first next time"; and from then on I always did.

Naturally, I had a longing for my parents. I remember lying in bed next to my grandmother at night and dreaming about having my own room inside my parents' apartment one day.

It is amazing to me – even as a psychologist now – to consider how those early experiences truly shape our lives and who we become.

One of my most delightful memories was from when I was nine years old and had started living with my parents again. My mother unexpectedly announced one day that she and my father were moving into a new apartment and I was to move in with them. I was so excited I couldn't sleep for a week.

My father now had a stable job working for one of his friend's companies as a custom's agent. He had also stopped drinking and gambling. My mother, who was an accountant, must have been keeping tabs for a while because when we arrived at our new apartment, we had a living room, a separate kitchen, a bedroom for me, and a bedroom for my parents. There was not a lot of furniture but it had everything we needed. It looked almost like it had in my dreams.

We even started to take an annual summer vacation to Marmaris on the coast in western Turkey. We would swim, sunbathe, walk the parks, bicycle, play ping-pong, hike in nature, you name it... Quite often, we stayed up until the sun rose, drove to the highest hill in the area – it was called "lovers' sight" – and broke warm bread with butter from the corner shop.

It was on one of those evenings that one of my friends, who has since become a famous musician, had a little too much to drink and decided to share how much he liked me. We were lying on a lounge chair by the pool, looking at the stars, and his words took me by surprise. When he realized I did not feel the same, he told me it was okay and asked me to give him a hug, saying "we will always be friends." I remember getting up, looking at him, and seeing the fear in his eyes, perhaps a bit of embarrassment and definitely some regret too. I remember then (1) feeling bad for him, (2) finding him powerless. I stood still for what was only a few moments, but actually felt like an eternity, and then – for whatever reason, I still to this day don't understand it – I turned my back on him and walked away.

It was such a small thing. Perhaps he forgot about it instantly, but the look in his eyes haunted me for months.

It hurt so much for so long that after a year or so, I woke one day from a nightmare and resolved to forgive myself. I made myself a promise, that whenever the opportunity presented itself, I would never turn down an act of kindness from anyone ever again.

■ ■ ■

"There exists a form of power and intelligence that represents the highest point of human potential," states Robert Greene in his book, *Mastery*. Arguably, it may be the ultimate source of greatest achievements, discoveries, and influences in human history. It is the kind of power and intelligence that is not consistently seen and is hardly ever found in our scholarly curricula; yet, it is the one that supports us most in our life journeys towards leadership.

The main problem with this form of power and intelligence is that, because we rarely experience it in full, and because we are not taught to detect it, it takes a lifetime of seeking to find it. At the same time, because it requires individuals to accept both our strengths and weaknesses, shadows and light sides, it demands us to keep an open heart to accept others for who they are, it is often misunderstood, easily ignored and/or commonly referred to as having no place in certain environments, like business.

Let us name this higher feeling *love* – the sensation of being "home", embodying an experience of being part of a greater reality. A sensation that offers the chance to detach from anxiety, as well as a feeling of deep connection.

You may recognize this love from an experience while you were carrying out a particular task. You may have felt at ease and like everything was flowing. You may recognize it from history, where some leaders have been described as observant and transcendent. You may recognize this love from being part of a community, where you may have always felt welcome… The truth is that this love is always available yet difficult to remain connected to at times. Not to mention it is a pity that the majority of us have been incorrectly taught about this love. Most of us carry a one-sided view of this love, associating it most closely to romanticism. That association with sexuality and attraction towards another human being is only short-cutting this love's true definition, shrinking its capacity and overlooking many years of experience embedded in rich culture and tradition.

This kind of love is a fundamental seed of our human experience and of belonging at large. Belonging is often defined as a unique and subjective experience that relates to a collection of internal and external motivators[15] (Rogers, 1951). The most common motivators include a yearning for connection and a need for recognition. In our experience, the key motivators of belonging are more holistic and better associated with the key elements of our human experience. For example, if you were to ask philosophers, theologians or socio-historical figures what it means to be "human", they would most likely share the following four components that make up our human experiences:

1. Physiology: Our bodily experience

2. Psychology: Our cognitive and behavioral experience

3. Sociology: Our spiritual and emotional experience

4. Ability: Our mental experience

---

15   https://link.springer.com/book/10.1007%2F978-981-10-5996-4

It is important that we recognize there has been more of an agreement on what makes up our human experience and the four listed components up until the 17th century. Today, when it comes to what it means to be a "human" and the definitions of our key experiences, we find more of an ideological division between different communities. That said, we still find that these descriptors fit with the science of "self-concept[16]" in modern psychology.

SELF-CONCEPT

Self-concept[17] is a "knowledge representation that contains knowledge about us, including our beliefs about our personality traits, physical characteristics, abilities, values, goals, and roles, as well as the knowledge that we exist as individuals".

Throughout our human development stages, we find that self-concept becomes more abstract and complex and is eventually organized into a variety of different cognitive aspects of the self, known as *self-schemas*. There comes a time in our child development process where we grow a perception of who we are, how we do things, who we become, etc. and these self-schemas[18] direct and inform our processing of self-relevant information (Harter, 1999) and largely affect our social cognition from there on in.

There are four key aspects to self-concept:

> 1. Self-reference. This relates to who we are at our core and our ability to naturally detect information relevant to ourselves. For example, we may think "I am too short" or "I am overweight". It refers to our physical quality and from there, shapes our experiences.

> 2. Personality identification. This relates to our perception of our specific and stable characteristics. For example, we may think "I

---

[16] https://opentextbc.ca/socialpsychology/chapter/the-cognitive-self-the-self-concept/

[17] https://opentextbc.ca/socialpsychology/chapter/the-cognitive-self-the-self-concept/

[18] https://open.lib.umn.edu/socialpsychology/chapter/4-1-the-cognitive-self-the-self-concept/

am outgoing" or "I am unfriendly". It refers to our psychological qualities and again, from there, shapes our experiences.

3. Social identification. This relates to our sense of self as a member of a community. For example, we may think "I am a mother"; and it impacts how we associate ourselves to others.

4. Condition. This relates to the perception we grow of the energy we find (un)available to do a particular task or challenge at a given moment. For example, we may think "I hate ironing" or "I love cooking"; whereas, in reality, we may take joy in ironing when we need to calm our mind, and we may dread the task of cooking if we have to do it three times a day.

Now comes the really interesting bit: Research[19] shows us that a sense of belonging "does not depend on participation with, or proximity to, others or groups; rather from a perception" of our qualities – the meaning we associate to our existence and the satisfaction we find through our social connections. This is the same for our sense of belonging to a place, to a group or to an event. Again, this is important because how we come to know ourselves and our qualities in relation to what we come in contact with actually shapes the sense of our belonging. Belonging, is, therefore, both an internal experience and a complex and dynamic process unique to each person's self-concept and their provided environment.

Though the idea of a need to belong has been recorded as having its roots in social psychology, and its measures clearly defined, there may be a more holistic view we can take on it – given the complexity and dynamism of a human system. According to Baumeister & Leary's conceptualization[20], which can be considered the most complete in current literature, fulfilling the need to belong involves satisfying two specific criteria. The first is around one's desire to have social contact. The second is around one's desire to share psychological states with one another. Again, this shows us the multi-faceted, interdependent,

---

19   https://www.researchgate.net/publication/225972964_Holistic_Human_Development
20   https://www.ncbi.nlm.nih.gov/pubmed/7777651/

and contextual ways of our becoming as humans. We use the word "holistic" consciously here because holism[21] is "an inclusive, meaning-centered, experience-focused" paradigm that emphasizes the connection necessary between intrinsic and extrinsic motivators that support our ways of being in life. Holistic thinking is then concerned with bridging the ego and self, individual and collective, human and technologies, offering a more balanced view and one grounded on sustainable development in support of our evolution. Non-dualistic in its mission, holism attempts to bridge the divide between mind and matter, individual and group, and artificial and natural, which have contributed to the psychic and spiritual fragmentation of meaning and purpose in postmodern society.

During a lifetime, every human being seeks to find some satisfying answers to their existence by asking themselves the questions:

- What do I look like?
- Who am I?
- Am I worthy?
- Am I capable?

This suggests that every human being has, therefore, an on-going need to be:

- *Seen* to satisfy one's physical needs
- *Heard* to satisfy one's psychological needs
- *Cared for* to satisfy one's social needs
- *Recognized for* their contribution to satisfy one's competence

Of course, it is possible to have simple positive relationships, thereby satisfying the need to interact and affiliate[22], yet we know a person may still not feel that they are fully accepted unless these specific needs are met in accordance with their expectations. In other words,

---

21   https://www.researchgate.net/publication/225972964_Holistic_Human_Development

22   https://www.ncbi.nlm.nih.gov/pmc/articles/PMC4685518/

Science of self-concept

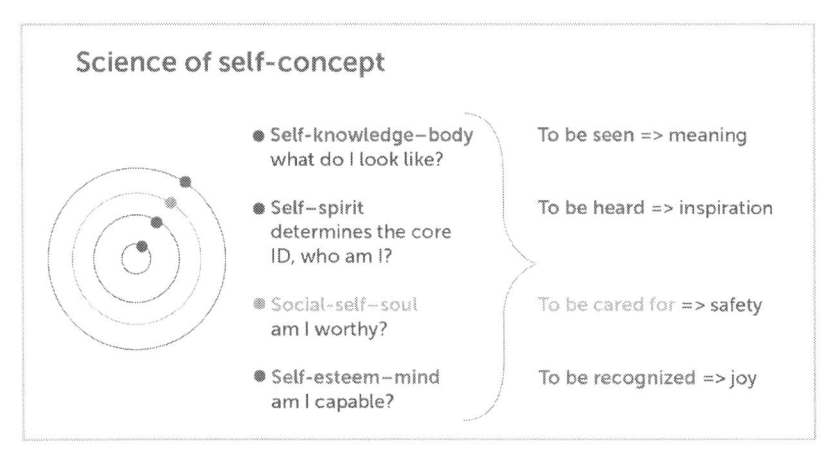

- Self-knowledge–body — what do I look like? → To be seen => meaning
- Self–spirit determines the core ID, who am I? → To be heard => inspiration
- Social–self–soul am I worthy? → To be cared for => safety
- Self-esteem–mind am I capable? → To be recognized => joy

Table 4. Self-Concept to Belonging

satisfying a general need for positive social interactions – for example, being part of a club or a workplace and not being treated differently – is not enough to guarantee the subjective experience for one's belonging[23].

This is exactly where we fail most often as leaders. While we each look for individual affirmation, we often struggle to connect to the kind of love described earlier and/or build the kind of inclusive environment that can support belonging. Interestingly, when we study leaders, we find that as children, most of them have experienced at least part of this kind of love, sometimes relying heavily on intuition. As children, we often have a better sense of who we are and can actively and clearly communicate our unique needs from a place of confidence. As adults, we often need to engage in a conscious (re-)discovery process to remember or catch a glimpse of who we truly are in order to develop an assertive and authentic way of communicating our unique needs.

This, too, is normal and closely related to the existential insecurities we grow while developing. For the majority of us, while we are developing, our daily anxieties start to form specific stories that shape the way we end up approaching things in life. Consciously or unconsciously, we choose to believe these stories that often break our

---

23 https://www.researchgate.net/publication/255959277_To_Belong_Is_to_Matter_Sense_of_Belonging_Enhances_Meaning_in_Life

confidence. As a result, we find comfort in looking elsewhere for our source of truth. We learn to distract ourselves by the sense of false belonging. Sometimes, we even become too self-identified with external powers such as title, position, company, etc. that eventually we lose complete connection from ourselves, others, and our surroundings.

The kind of act in violation of language or misconduct in behavior observed becomes a by-product, an outcome of that inner fragmentation. One person's suffering and inability to access love becomes a disabler for others' ability to experience connection. When we are broken into a million pieces inside and/or unable to collect our pieces together, we incapacitate ourselves by avoidance. In this state, we tend to build barriers to hide behind and/or to keep others out. We choose to sit and stew in our negative thoughts or emotions or bottle it up and pretend without allowing any chance to heal.

Inside today's workplaces, this has become the default starting point for how the majority of us behave, relate to, and work with one another. It is no wonder we are struggling to achieve effectiveness, collaboration, and innovation from our efforts. What is concerning is not the current state as much as our lack of acknowledgment. It seems that not only do the majority of us struggle to put our best self forward, but we also have no idea which theologies or mindsets may serve us better and help us change our behavior.

The kind of sustainable growth in business that's needed and the kind of exemplary behavior to change calls for a *transcendental leadership* and an evolution of our ways of "being", "relating", and "doing". Each one of us needs to grow skills to notice self-patterns, and mental distance to reflect upon experiences and to develop awareness. Only then can we learn new techniques to regenerate our energy and actively engage in rebuilding our skills. In a world where we continue to undermine the power of science and arts, where we continue to disown personal (individual) accountability, and disengage in cross-boundary cooperation, we are bound to see more issues that raise and affect our humanities over the years. For example, scientists and researchers have been warning us about the potential of a world-wide pandemic for 20 years. In the absence of dedicated focus and funding, only 17 years after SARS and 10 years after Swine Flu, we find ourselves in a more threatening situation with COVID-19. At the start of the pandemic, the scientists were ignored/dismissed as overreacting. Then we saw individuals not taking personal accountability by flouting measures, and we saw countries closing their borders and fighting over supplies. The way forward is to be found in our collective ability to build trust, listen actively and with humility to those who carry wisdom and foresight, and to stand on a united foundation of values; and that is highly dependent on our individual ability to connect to the love available to us and at a much deeper, intuitive level.

BEING

In his book, *Man's Search for Meaning*, Viktor Frankl proposed that humans are driven to find meaning in life, and he termed this motivation "will to meaning." Klinger (2012) argues that "the human brain cannot sustain purposeless living," because all the systems of the brain were designed by nature to facilitate meaningful thought and action. Similarly, the modern-day philosopher and author Roman Krznaric writes in his book *How to Find Fulfilling Work*, "We have entered a new age of fulfillment, in which the great dream is to trade up from money to meaning."

Indeed, meaning at large is what each one of us are looking for. Meaning-making[24] is the way we understand life. It is the process by which we construe, relate, and make sense of our comings. As human beings, we care equally about understanding the *why* of something as much as the *what*. More importantly, consciously or not, we notice the *how*. The *how* works its way inside of us, into our bodily systems, and mixes with our soul to evolve into the culture of our make-up. The *how* becomes the igniter to our *why*. The *how* vastly shapes the way our experiences are formed. Think of it this way... While it may

---

24   https://www.wikiwand.com/en/Meaning-making

be true that the desire for material success is still widespread across our societies, we actually understand deep inside that pots of gold do not always equate to our sustained health or joy. Yet, we continue to work harder – better, faster, stronger – in reach of them. Why do we do this? Why do we disregard our knowledge and experience? We do it because our sense of *how* offers us the perspective that to be respected and recognized, we have to work harder than others.

This is an extremely critical point because while we may or may not be in favor of the broader system we are part of, we need to understand that how we realize our life mission – which beliefs, mindsets, emotions we carry, assumptions we work with, and behaviors we display to relate to others – impacts the formation of our cultures. Contrary to the common perception, we are not separate from the environment, the system, the culture or even the workplaces we are part of; rather, we make up the environment, the system, the culture.

It is a huge mistake then that when we refer to our human-ness today, we rarely consider ourselves as part of a bigger creation. This sort of disconnected view undermines the complete set of our intrinsic needs and our desire to be a part of holistic experiences. The kind of elitist intellect we have given power to over the centuries has grown in us a false sense of superiority and given us isolation in return. As a result, we find ourselves in a vicious circle of perceptual loss. We no longer slow down to consciously consider how our cells work; how our nervous systems get activated; how our organs communicate with one another; how our thoughts evolve; our emotions; or how our behaviors might be awakened as a result of these cycles. These are the kind of reflective questions we avoid asking ourselves and each other; therefore, the majority of the time we have no idea where we stand consciously – whether we are above or below the line of consciousness to begin with...

Before dying at the age of 39, Blaise Pascal compiled a collection of thoughts, which were later published as *Pascal's Pensees*[25]. One of his thought-provoking statements reads, "All of humanity's prob-

---

25   https://www.amazon.com/Pascals-Pensées-Blaise-Pascal-ebook/

lems stem from man's inability to sit quietly in a room alone." Pascal claimed our fear of silence is what leads us into a false sense of comfort in life. Indeed, though it may be easier to hide behind things like job title or status, and to live a life pursued by others – especially in a world full of distractions where we are constantly fed ideas of what good means – in reality we are creatures of "being" by virtue of our livingness and vitality. We can certainly influence where we stand, but first, we must come to terms with the implications of what we have chosen.

When it comes to self-knowledge and telling one's story, we need to understand that if we are not connected to the kind of unbiased, compassionate, and unifying love as described, that we will continue to grow a false connection to our story based on someone else's measures (failures, accomplishments, "shortcomings"). Not only will this continue to diminish the power of our unique story as individuals, it will also support an uneven playing field for collective growth and formation of potential new ways of being, relating, and doing work inside our workplaces. Furthermore, when we borrow our story from others, we allow ourselves to be manipulated by the value we place on them. This sort of outlook motivates a sense of "competition" in us. Any form of competition is hostile when it comes to leadership practice. Arguing that one has to be better than another drives individuals to look for ways to differentiate themselves by drawing on differences. This creates a cycle of sickness, where the individual self-motivates to work towards a definition of "success", that is not *their* definition, and then they even impose the same definition on others. Our brain processes information best through contrasts, and our egos love praise, but it is really the recognition of one's dignity – the factual observation of effort rather than a value judgment – that motivates us. The tendency to connect to someone else's story, then, ends up shrinking our capacity and diminishes our ability to develop respect for ourselves and others.

If we want to evolve our way of *being*, it is imperative we start paying attention to how we frame our life stories, how (often) we live in the moment, and how we exercise connection. Our life stories provide context for our experiences. Our consciousness begins when our brains gain power over our personal narratives. Our hearts open when we choose to connect. Transcendence requires us to see transformative effects hidden inside our life experiences, and to pursue the journey as a way of discovering our identity and creating meaning[26].

RELATING

Relatedness[27] is often described as the essence of kinship between two individuals. Inside organizations, how information and knowledge flows and how we work with information to create new ideas, concepts, and schemas, as well as how we share knowledge to make decisions, are primary functions of relatedness. Although many organizations tend to lead with collaboration to enable innovation, relatedness is a better moderator on our way to collaborative behavior[28] (The Oxford Handbook of Entrepreneurship and Collaboration p. 615). Furthermore, the psychological underpinnings of how different people relate to one another inside of an environment are often the most important factors in better understanding the specific barriers to organizational and societal issues.

Though relatedness is one of our key primary motivators as human beings, we like to assume we are often objective in how we relate to others. But our behaviors stem from our ideologies and get shaped by our social perceptions; therefore, we are far more subjective in our relationships than we would ever think. I often say that if there is a good reason for what you believe and what you do, then you may be rational; but we need to remember there are many ways of knowing and interpreting what is rational. If we dare to look at our collective ways of thinking, we would actually see that we are completely irrational in the sense of what is rational to one is not rational to an-

26 https://www.researchgate.net/publication/255959277_To_Belong_Is_to_Matter_Sense_of_Belonging_Enhances_Meaning_in_Life
27 https://www.sciencedirect.com/topics/psychology/relatedness
28 https://www.oxfordhandbooks.com/view/10.1093/oxfordhb/9780190633899.001.0001/oxfordhb-9780190633899

other. Different facts lead to different truths and they are also often different depending on the unique learning we gain from a given experience. Because of these differences, and especially when disconnected from love, we must pay attention to the possibility of growing emotional bias.

An emotional bias[29] can be best understood as a distortion in cognition. Recent experiments in neuroscience have shown how emotions and cognition, which are present in different areas of the brain (and work together), can interfere with each other during decision-making processes, often leading to emotions taking over reasoning[30]. The bias can be towards the positive or negative, but either way it distorts the neutrality of having perspective; and it is also highly influenced by the stresses of ambiguity and volatility in our current environments. Many working professionals suffer from this state of mind. Especially those who have been through traumatic early life experiences learn to draw on negative story building that often replays its image back onto them. This tendency both exhausts individual capacity and challenges moral decision making. When operating from a place of bias, we both deplete our energy sources and reduce the possibility of acting more authentically, making ourselves unable to manage interpersonal differences with others.

Relating without an emotional bias, on the other hand, requires us to have access to other people's thoughts and beliefs in addition to our own. We tend to look inwards to our own beliefs, thoughts, and emotions in judging our bias, and outwards to others' actions for judging their bias. Because biases generally operate unconsciously, we often cannot really see our bias even when looking inwards. This dichotomy is a basic aspect of our human cognition and often fuels the disagreements and conflict between people.

If we are serious about finding more effective ways of relating and working together, we must invest in gaining awareness to overcome our bias, prejudice, and stereotyping. This is a complex process – sim-

---

29 https://www.wikiwand.com/en/Emotional_bias
30 https://www.ncbi.nlm.nih.gov/pmc/articles/PMC5573739/

ilar to how we develop our sense of being, it requires us to become more *attentive* to our verbal, behavioral, and affective cues while we are relating. In our current working environments where we are running from one thing to another without time to so much as catch our breaths, this is almost impossible.

That said, compassionate empathy is a great learning tool for activating this kind of connection.

Compassionate empathy[31] is about allowing someone else's feelings and needs to inhabit our consciousness without those feelings/needs taking over our consciousness. It is like being a "soul-mate" to someone by walking in their shoes and seeing the world through their glasses for a particular period of time. Instead of creating patterns that distance ourselves from others – patterns that "protect" us from what we think we want from a relationship – by putting parties in a mutual state of fear, compassionate empathy opens the door to relative intimacy, setting the stage for trust and shared vulnerability. Since we are often dealing with intellectual and cultural processes inside our work environments, the key to activating compassionate empathy may be in remembering that there exists no opportunity of collaboration without neutrality. It is only when we relate to one another from a neutral standpoint that we become able to avoid our natural desire to control, and capable to engage in conflict productively.

DOING

When we are hooked on a particular emotional bias, our most natural default is the most common modus operandi: self-interest. Growing a sense of "otherness", meaning feeling different from other people, which is a thought or self-perception that's often fed by feelings of isolation and loneliness, we immediately fall back on traditional forms of control seeking. This is a dangerous space because when we self-isolate, we prevent ourselves from receiving input. We need to hear information and receive signals of validation and violation

---

31   https://link.springer.com/article/10.1007/s11245-019-09636-7

from those we socialize with to continue building healthy boundaries. Without this, we grow doubtful of our worth and further hesitate to share our vulnerabilities. In our defense, we work hard to preserve the status quo in pursuit of self-protection, further decreasing the chances of production and output, and in turn enforcing a climate of fear and despair.

This mode of operating highly impacts our *doing* inside organizations – the way we engage in different activities. Doing is a way of ordering things for ourselves inside a given environment. As human beings, we like things to be categorized and systematized. We do this, partially because we are looking for order, but also because we don't always feel that we know what is the "right" thing to do exactly. When we know what we are responsible for, when we are clear on the purpose, what is valued, the routines we can put into practice, the stories we can tell, the networks we can navigate through, etc., we feel significantly better about how we are contributing.

Understanding how we behave and work together, and its contribution to culture formation, has a direct link to our organizational productivity measures. There is an expansive new body of evidence spanning psychology, neuroscience, and even economics, revealing that when we are able to relate to others effectively, our physiology improves for the better. When our physiology improves, our emotional state improves, and with the right conditions, our spiritual state improves as a result. In a holistic state of authenticity and serenity, we become better geared towards innovation. From there, our productivity flourishes.

In the workplace, it is largely related to what one sees/observes in a particular setting and about their perceived reflection[32]. During shared experiences, partial or intermittent negative reinforcements can create an effective climate of fear and doubt[33] as does absence of values or not acting in accordance to defined values, and lack of

---

32   http://ncsce.net/wp-content/uploads/2016/10/Finlay-2008-Reflecting-on-reflective-practice-PBPL-paper-52.pdf

33   https://www.wikiwand.com/en/Doubt

the right motivational mechanisms. Several academic studies over the years have confirmed a relationship between bullying and fear and between bullying and an autocratic leadership or authoritarian ways of settling conflicts[34]. From the scientific evidence[35], we find that the style in which we manage our day-to-day operations, make decisions, and handle conflict can greatly contribute to the formation of a climate of fear. Inside environments where there is not enough inclusivity in brainstorming, not enough room for a dialogue, not enough constructivism in handling conflict, and not enough positive language or storytelling, we find that fear states rise.

It is imperative to say a few words on the climate of fear, here, because it is one of the most detrimental things to forming and developing productive individuals, teams, and organizations. Fear is a feeling induced by perceived danger or threat. A culture of fear[36] is a concept, largely popularized by American sociologist Barry Glassner. It is used for describing behaviors that incite fear in the general population to achieve certain goals and/or to ignite motivation through use of emotional bias. Amy Edmondson, an American scholar who has studied teaming and psychological safety at large, reports finding that better performing teams make more errors than worse performing ones[37]. She refers to this state as having an "openness" in the environment, in which people are not only invited to the conversation and to contribute but they are welcome to admit making mistakes and/or false assumptions. More recent studies show that fear may also result from the overall sense of change that a place is undergoing or when someone joins a new area. A new employee, for example, may feel fearful as they lack familiarity and knowledge of a given domain. The truth is that fear goes way beyond the conditions of one's work content, position or the workplace setting offered. It is more of a reflection of an organizational state and is highly depen-

---

34   https://www.wikiwand.com/en/Workplace_conflict
35   https://www.ncbi.nlm.nih.gov/pmc/articles/PMC3835442/
36   https://www.wikiwand.com/en/Culture_of_fear
37   https://www.researchgate.net/publication/229748544_Group_Behavior_and_Performance

dent on how people see one another and create a culture of work in a given environment.

On the other hand, we know that people who work in a culture where they "feel free to express affection, tenderness, care, and compassion for one another" are more satisfied with their jobs, committed to the organization, and accountable for their performance[38].

So, *how* we work matters equally; and it becomes an informer for how we best structure our resources, the processes, procedures, facilities, and/or technologies we leverage.

RECONNECTING TO LOVE

Love of work... Love of nature... Love of cooking... Love of patriarchy...

Our experience of love comes in a variety of ways, shapes, colors, and conditions. The kind of love we have been describing in this chapter is one and whole in its essence. There is no categorical difference to its substance. It is rooted and spacious at the same time. It is infinite and immortal. It is unique in its ability to be always available to us.

If we want to be loving with one another, however; if we want to remain connected to this kind of love, share it with one other, and engage in its creative power, then we must know who we are before we come to know any other. This process of *self-esteem development* entails getting clarity on our life purpose, understanding our uniqueness, growing self-knowledge, and awareness of our blind spots, to respect, accept, and claim ourselves as a whole and valuable entity; because only then can we truly "see" – respect and accept – and create space for others as the unique individuals that they are.

In scientific terms, there are two parts to self-esteem: (1) Confidence in our ability to think and to cope with the challenges of life, (2) Confidence in our right to exist, to be worthy, deserving, and to be successful. Most of us do better in the first part of that definition than the second, but we do need both to develop a healthy dose. This

---

38   https://hbr.org/2014/01/employees-who-feel-love-perform-better

is when we become able to present ourselves authentically and without fear of attribution and/or differentiated treatment across different environments, finding and offering belonging to others.

This kind of love also requires us to remain connected to reality, and this is hard. This is also why many philosophers and poets speak to the fact that love is learned. This kind of love requires us to practice caring about others, remain tuned into the broader environment to observe what's going on around us, and exercise an active will to learn our way to neutrality. It calls on us individually to make space for reflection, to grow comfort around discomfort, and to actively notice what may not be intuitive for us. Again, grounding ourselves in reality and core values is particularly harder today because there is so much noise in the system. Everywhere we turn, there is someone prettier, smarter, with a better car, better title. The picture depicted and projected – especially through social media – in society often transforms us into a movie-setting, in which we get to be the extras playing the smaller parts. Perspective-taking, here, can become an important skill. When busy, we often relate from a place of reaction, rather than reflection or a neutral ground of understanding.

This kind of love also involves responsibility in that language can serve as another powerful tool. The kind of words and expressions we use have a power over us and how we come to see the world. It is a fact that we take language for granted. We grow comfortable in our limited vocabulary and do not show interest in expanding the ways we express ourselves. By doing so, we limit ourselves. For example, when we feel scared of losing our credibility in a team meeting or when we observe a colleague in a sad situation, we say "I am stressed." But being "stressed" is not the same as being scared or feeling sad for someone else, so the words we choose to use here do not tell the full story. Sometimes we overtly lie because we do not want to offend anybody or come off as needy, mean, demanding or confrontational. Other times, we covertly lie because we are afraid of what people will think of us if we tell the truth, or that they will not deliver (and therefore, disappoint us), or take away something we have (perhaps a material possession or image we have worked hard to create and maintain).

It has been reported by Brene Brown that the majority of us think that honesty is about keeping facts straight when sharing with another person. This is one part of its definition. Another part is about staying true to our way of being, acting in coherence with our core values, and honoring our human needs. By being clear about our needs, we accept the reality of how we feel and create a choice to alleviate our own suffering before it hurts someone else. When we fall into the habit of exaggerating or partially acknowledging our emotions, we tend to get stuck, and often find ourselves alternating between being a horrible person or a saint. As a consequence, we never see others equal to ourselves – we either feel superior or inferior.

Finally, this kind of love is unapologetic and forgiving in that gratitude can serve as a great affirmation of its goodness. Through different life experiences, our choice to exercise gratitude presents itself as a gift of affirmation that there is good and bad in the world and either way, we are better for the experience. Knowing what we appreciate in life points to our self-knowledge, but paying attention[39] to what we feel grateful for shifts ourselves into a positive frame of mind. This state drives up our wellbeing and can serve as a foundational ground for employee fulfillment through positive reinforcement and sharing. In other words, gratitude not only allows us to celebrate the present and what life has to offer, it also blocks negative emotions in the body and helps us grow a higher sense of worth. Over the years, many studies have been conducted on the power of gratitude. Some[40] studied individuals whose wellbeing was increased by practicing gratitude, and others[41] studied individuals whose ill-being was elevated as a result of gratitude exercises. Either way, research[42] clearly demonstrates that

---

39 https://www.psychologytoday.com/us/basics/attention
40 https://greatergood.berkeley.edu/topic/gratitude/definition#why_practice
41 https://greatergood.berkeley.edu/article/item/how_gratitude_changes_you_and_your_brain
42 https://greatergood.berkeley.edu/pdfs/GratitudePDFs/6Emmons-BlessingsBurdens.pdf

focusing on what we are grateful for is a universally rewarding way to feel happier. It makes us feel connected and fulfilled, and develops in us the capacity to forgive.

Business is no longer an island; nor is leadership. Most of us need others to succeed and we seek empathy and kindness to engage with one another. The kind of transformative leadership we want to awaken inside our organizations is not about one's achievement of a title, a goal or prestige, it is about one's transcendence. When we can connect to this kind of unconditional, unbiased love, we can see ourselves clearly and relate to others not only as human beings, but also as equal species, having shared hopes, cares, needs, disappointments, etc.

Sometimes we wonder if our single way of "being" or "doing" can really make a difference when there is so much insecurity, disintegration, fear, and doubt already present in the world. Let me assure you that where you ground yourself truly matters. This is the most important step in organizational psychology, in culture evolution, and the most important factor in social contagion. Another research[43], published in *Psychological Science*, a journal of the Association for Psychological Science, indicates that we have more power over the design of a system than we think, because we are social learners. In other words, we learn best by observing what others do. Nature does not really have what we would call a "mind" of its own, nor a specific project for us. It cannot tell us what to do; only we can. The climates we collectively create as leaders are a direct reflection of today, and in turn, these shared climates color the way we will develop as individuals in the future.

Hatred feeds hatred, fear feeds fear, and love feeds love. If you are in a seat of power, I wish that you find the courage to connect and lead out of this higher sense of power and intelligence that draws upon your most authentic way of showing while maximizing your capacity to care, to connect, and to cultivate. When in doubt, ask yourself if you are disclaiming, diving, excluding, differentiating in the name of

---

43   https://www.psychologicalscience.org/news/releases/diminishing-fear-vicariously-by-watching-others.html

love of <fill in the blanks>. Because if you are, you can be sure you are not driven by love, as love is always invisible, intuitive, and inclusive. Love is a quality of respect and eliminating boundaries.

Because we always have a choice, I choose love.

PART 2

BEHAVIORS & MINDSETS

I was 13 years old when I lost my father in a traffic accident and my world flipped upside down. I felt lost, disappointed, confused, and frustrated. I withdrew from friendships, and after a steady decline in desire to learn, also extracurricular activities.

One day a month after the event, I was sitting alone at my desk, looking out the window during a lunch break and writing poems, and one of my teachers walked in. She asked how I was doing. I said "fine". She pulled a chair up next to me, handed me a glass of water, and started rubbing my back lightly. After a few minutes, I couldn't stop the tears rolling down my cheeks.

"I want to drop out", I said, "I no longer want to become a brain surgeon and nobody loves me." She lifted up my chin with her soft hands and said, "That's too bad because I have a brother who has brain development problems and I was hoping you would become one of the best doctors to help him. And", she continued, "I love you very much. You are one of our best students."

I looked up to her face and was completely taken aback by her sincerity.

I never forgot the immediate feeling of warmth that suddenly took over my heart and, from there, my whole body.

That evening, I announced to my mother that I was going to study abroad.

LEADERSHIP REDEFINED, ONE HUMAN AT A TIME!

Over the years I have come to know and work with hundreds of executives.

Some of these executives have tried very hard to do everything right on paper, and yet, their employees still do not feel committed to them. Some executives struggled with the experience of having to manage a relatively mid-level turnover for sustainable periods of time. Others failed in driving transformative change because they were acting more like a manager than a leader, despite the position they had been asked to fulfill. It is notable that many of these executives were actually promoted into people leadership roles because they were very successful at managing work at an individual level. In many cases, it was either that the company did not have a technical career track to promote these senior individual contributors; in other cases, the senior individual contributors themselves saw a managerial position as a way to advance their career status inside the company. In either case, even as senior contributors, very few of them understood what it actually means to become a leader of others. Very few had the passion for coaching others, or the skill set and tested capacity necessary to achieve what the role actually requires.

Leadership today is commonly defined as the state or the position of providing an opportunity for action. In its current (and economical) terms, leadership is closely related to *doing*. Leaders are seen as unique in their ability to manage complexity. They are believed to execute on strategies exceptionally well. They are assumed to hire and build extraordinary teams. When we think of a leader, we imagine a super-human able to drive change while constantly keeping a good handle on day-to-day operations. The feeling we have for a leader is often masculine. We imagine them to be tough and durable. Their impact we assume should be measured by profit-making performance indicators. The question is: Are the organizational leaders we know – business or otherwise – really all that? Do the majority of leaders we recognize really carry all those attributes we imagine? Or, is the profile we create in our minds more a portrayal of a unicorn, and perhaps one we wish to become some day?

As an example, let's take George (not his real name), the CEO of a technology start-up who was promoted because of his technical depth and who was never asked whether he aspired to lead people. Or Sakine (name changed), a VP of marketing in a multinational who accepted the leadership role as a way to advance her career because she was unsure whether there would ever be another path available to her. You might think we are only picking "poor" examples. Close your eyes for a second and consider a leader you know or recognize well based on the models present in our society: Imagine a country president, for example, or an institution head, or your chief executive officer. What does your heart tell you about this person's core intent for keeping their seat? Do you imagine the person having the capabilities and the capacity necessary to lead and inspire others? Do you envision the person becoming a role model for guiding moral, societal behavior? Would you want your children to be inspired by them?

Through promotions, we elevate people to particular roles. But we do not often see the hidden agenda they have going on: To use their position, responsibilities, and actions to further their own success. So in promoting them, we actually offer a disservice to the others that will look up to them as a leader. When we automatically promote strong performers into people leadership roles without taking into account their preparation and/or collecting evidence on their sustained role modeling inside our organizations, we end up sharing a message that makes the "what" of someone's *doing* more important than the "why" of someone's way of *being*. This feeds our subconscious with a separation between the morality of "how" we do – our way of *relating* – and "what" we are *doing*.

Naturally, those in followership experience a state of confusion. They see the kind of organizational values posted on the values that support the "how", and the kind of behaviors demonstrated and rewarded by the leaders, and they find a mismatch. For example, one of the corporate values listed may be "trust". An employee seeing this would naturally expect there to be a certain level of psychological safety and transparency. If they find, however, that information is not being shared openly or they see people getting punished for speaking up, it will lead to confusion. In understanding the common leadership behaviors, they rationalize that it must be most important to do well as a leader. The followers, then, look up to the people behind the role – not the actual role – to drive key action. From there, they start modeling the same kind of behaviors. The majority of followers will also take the stance of feeding the leader – through their interactions – what they think may be better, faster, more creative in order to contribute to broader success. This puts the whole organization in a state of constant action and in support of behaviors that may or may not be representative of core organizational values. "I must work harder and longer hours to gain my next promotion". This is the mindset we find most incapacitated working professionals to have. People literally sacrifice their energy and values to mimic what they perceive to be behaviors of their leaders and of organizational recognition, and often without taking into consideration the impact of their action – on themselves or on the broader organization.

This state of constant action not only drives disintegration among an organization's different units. Over time, it also feeds into the ego of those in the provided leadership roles. Those who have been selected as leaders inside an organization either build an impression around why they must be where they are in the first place or slowly begin to forget their core mission of serving others. They literally overlook the core purpose of their intended leadership, whatever personal or otherwise philosophy they may have, and start to correlate their achievement to what they perceive may have gotten them there in the first place. Therefore, they continue playing by the rules they believe to be right, and slowly begin to grow a personal interest in keeping the status quo. In the majority of these scenarios, we find leaders eventually get into a disjointed state of mind and disconnect from reality. Many develop a slightly different persona – sometimes withdrawn, more often aggressive. As heart-breaking as this reality is, we must recognize that this is only a human pattern of response.

Imagine yourself being tapped for a people leadership role because you are able to achieve results through your individual contribution year after year. Imagine suddenly that your peers, colleagues, and employees have a more elevated perception of your status and achievement. Imagine feeling deep inside that you are not ready to handle such authority and power. Yet, imagine that the organization continues to reward you for your results and others slowly start to mimic your behaviors.

If you are someone who is not trained to find balance between the positive and negative sides of your *being*; if you are not trained to access your emotions and attentively listen to others from that authentic place; if you are not trained to consciously keep your capacities in check in times of stress, it will only be a matter of time before you find yourself getting more and more rigid in your way of working as you start needing to survive one of the most complex jobs you have ever had. Just like the leaders we serve and work with, you, too, will start to take comfort in familiar ways of working. You, too, will look for increased authority through the boundaries, policies, procedures, and protocols that you established yourself. You, too, will focus on doing the bare minimum, ticking the box, and considering that a success, rather than really reaching your potential. You, too, will enjoy the recognition that comes with it. When you get there, if you care to look around, you will even find that some keep up better with your ways of working than others, which will prompt all kinds of new assumptions for you. Before you know it, you will start believing that you indeed deserve your position, and start viewing those "others" as not so worthy. That is when you will start developing a sense of fake confidence, the kind of confidence that is not grounded in the kind of love we described earlier, but rather in others' respect and fear.

It is an unfortunate fact that our brains cannot differentiate between what is imagined and what is real. It is a scientific fact that the brain will always default to what it is most familiar with. Once we are convinced of something, even if it is not real, we will eventually become convinced of our ways of thinking, unaware of the impact we bring upon ourselves and our surroundings. This is a vicious loop and one that is very hard to get out of once in it. This is typically the point when followers start to recognize the leader's pattern of behavior, and sometimes even find the courage to question their standards.

When we look at the etymology of leading, however, we see a slightly different meaning than the one we have adopted over the years. The original definition of leadership presents a guide – an educator to a particular flow or process. With this definition, there is a strong focus on the link between the leader and the follower. There is an understanding of interconnectedness. There is a service aspect, meaning there is separation between the position and the person and a comprehension that the role is designed to serve something bigger than the leader themselves – like a unifying mission. There is also a focus on the shared power in this definition. Even though authority is granted to a particular person, there is acknowledgment that the "real" power of the organization is shared equally across all of its key stakeholders.

The beauty of this definition is that it introduces the possibility of a strong link between what we do, how we relate, and who we become. With that, it is more holistic, and provides a better fit for our complex human condition. The thing about our human physiology is that our brains and hearts pulsate together. If you would ever observe open brain surgery, you would see that the two organs have the same rhythm. What is not visible, however, is that when one of these organs goes at a hundred miles per hour, the other tries to adjust, no matter the cost. Therefore, for the majority of our current leaders living via their brain most of the time, believing they will only be cared for and rewarded based on their bottom-line results, their hearts and bodies try to compensate, leading to severe fragmentation and imbalance.

The good news is that, when we are able to help these leaders gain clarity about their identity and support them in the process of intent purification, we find that they begin to become whole again in the way they see themselves, what their purpose is, and the way to approach it, and we see an immediate upturn in their wellbeing. Similarly, repeated observations in the "Absence Management Report, CIPD, 2016[44]" on health and wellbeing show that employees who can access and experience emotional support at work are more than two times more likely to live longer than employees who cannot access or do not have an emotionally supportive workplace. Remaining whole and having high-quality human connections is also beneficial for others. According to "Effects of Positive Practices on Organizational Effectiveness[45]" research by Cameron et al. at the University of Michigan, when leaders adopt a human-centered view of business, and create cultures grounded in respect, trust, and compassion, the performance of the organization rises along with the wellbeing of the individual.

When I think of the current state of human evolution and the kind of future environments we need to support our sustained development, I find the concept of leadership quickly getting closer to its original definition. The future of leadership is about someone taking full accountability in finding and unleashing potential and having the capacity to build organizational environments of compassion and wisdom. In that, I find leadership to be decreasingly less related to "doing" something well and increasingly more related to "being" a certain way – to driving a journey forward. I find it a concept no longer limited to the few or to those with a natural talent to serve others. I find leadership an enabling force, in which a leader and a follower share power, and decisions can be co-owned to the equal benefit of everyone.

Similarly, I consider preparing the next generation of leaders inside a corporation to be a shared responsibility between the individual and the organization. Only then, I believe, can we imagine working

---

44 https://www.cipd.co.uk/Images/absence-management_2016_tcm18-16360.pdf
45 https://deepblue.lib.umich.edu/bitstream/handle/2027.42/83259/Cameron,%20Mora,%20&%20Leutscher%20-%20Effects%20of%20Positive%20Practices%20on%20Organizational%20Performance%20-%20Revised%20Submission.pdf?sequence=1

in organizations where all people, despite their demographics, background, education or income levels, experience an equal opportunity for dignity, psychological endurance, and justice. Only then, I believe, can we imagine working in a climate motivated by meaning, inspiration, safety, and joy, that offers recognition for people's true and unique contribution – not compared to someone else's. Only then, I believe, can we imagine being led by individuals who are not only connected to their life's goals but can also lead consciously and with presence, supporting growth. Only then, I believe, can we collectively awaken our consciousness to understand the value of common human motivations, and honor everyone's unique right to development on our way to sustainable productivity.

This is the very reason we decided to study hundreds of long lasting organizations and their leadership behaviors together with Stanford University's Center for Compassion Altruistic Research and Education (CCARE). Over the course of two years, we looked in depth at ~40% of the Fortune 500 organizations to understand what it may mean to be a leader in this increasingly complex, highly digitized and challengingly interconnected world. And what it may take to build more human-centric organizations without losing their focus on productivity.

Specifically, we engaged in two activities:

> 1. Surveying 118 organizations with enduring qualities in phases to collect, analyze, and interpret both quantitative and qualitative data to identify high-level, established trends. We explored the kind of questions that can offer us insight and help us re-consider the original terms of leadership. For example, we probed on the following (and more):

> - What does it take to build sustainable growth in your organization?
> - What is the core of your organizational abilities?
> - Who is considered a "leader" inside your organization?
> - What does it mean to be a leader (and not)?

- Which knowledge and skill(s) are prerequisites to becoming a leader?

- Which knowledge and skill(s) are successful in driving change?

- Which mindset(s) and behavior(s) are successful in leading oneself (and others)?

- What sorts of inside-out interventions can we explore to create work environments that draw out the best in others?

2. Conducting a meta-analysis of existing, scientific research from globally credible institutions (i.e. University of Michigan, McGill University, Stanford, and Harvard Universities, etc.). We drew on research from several disciplines including neuroscience, positive psychology, the biology of wellbeing, organizational psychology, and sociology. We examined the way individuals process information, what enables their particular behaviors, and the effects of a large variety of core human attributes.

The Path
Together with Stanford University, we studied ~120 Fortune 500 companies that stayed in the game since 2000.

Adaptability + Resilience = Sustainable Growth

Behaviors	
	Leaders sit in many chairs
	Leaders lead themselves
	Leaders lead for head, heart, hand
	Leaders lead for connection
	Leaders lead with growth
Mindsets	
	Caring
	Abundance
	Wellbeing
	...
	Growth
Core Human Attributes	
	Purpose
	Courage
	...
	Mastery

Table 5. The Path To Sustainable Growth

Our findings represent a re-discovery towards core human attributes and specific organizational development experiences that has proven to equip organizations with new capability and leaders with expanded capacity. While some forces of change, such as digitalization, are a major trend today, our research validates that organizations are still going to get the most competitive advantage from their people. It is equally important to note that the organizations we looked into are also organizations that reported a number of positive outcomes over other Fortune 500 companies such as a lower burnout rate, reduced absences, higher levels of teamwork, higher safety ratings, and a deeper sense of personal accountability for work performance.

ENABLING SUSTAINABLE GROWTH – A DIFFERENT ECONOMICAL MODEL

Through our research, we were able to confirm that enduring businesses that make it through unprecedented volatility, ambiguity, and change go way beyond a singular goal of meeting financial targets. They connect to a sense of purpose, invest in building a culture, reach for a differentiated employee experience, and activate energy in leaders to leverage beyond the more typical ways of rewarding employees, like bonuses, extra benefits, or even investment in the office environment. For these businesses, sustainable growth is as much about the outcome as it is about a way of living.

During the research analysis, we discovered two specific factors that enabled organizations to engage in sustainable growth:

1. Adaptability: The organizations' *capability* to evolve its processes, procedures, etc.

2. Resilience: The individuals' *capacity* to bounce back and recover from adversity.

In understanding the specific drivers for adaptability and resilience, we discovered five non-traditional leadership behaviors that lift up an organization, and a number of new mindsets in support of these behaviors. Finally, we discovered eight core human attributes that serve as inner motivators to either enable or disable the creation of a positive working climate. Furthermore, we found that if and when leaders can tap into those core human attributes, and do so in combination with the mindsets discovered, they not only exhibit the leadership behaviors listed, but also drive positive impact on the culture and overall performance of an organization.

During the meta-analysis of existing research, we discovered two equally important pieces of data:

1. Self-Esteem & Trust Has A Positive Impact

One of the discoveries was that when individuals are invested and have a healthy self-esteem, they are able to build lasting relationships, which in turn has a positive impact on their vitality. A quick snapshot of outcomes experienced when employees are grounded in self-esteem from Paul J. Zak's study can be found in Table 6 below.

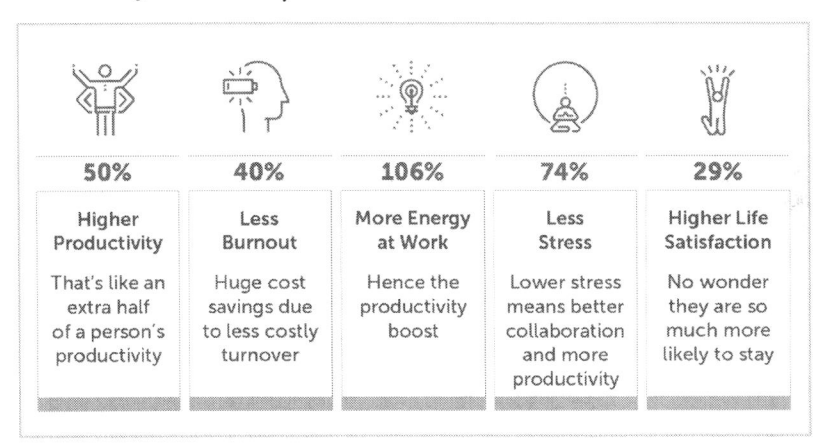

50%	40%	106%	74%	29%
Higher Productivity	Less Burnout	More Energy at Work	Less Stress	Higher Life Satisfaction
That's like an extra half of a person's productivity	Huge cost savings due to less costly turnover	Hence the productivity boost	Lower stress means better collaboration and more productivity	No wonder they are so much more likely to stay

Table 6. Employees Grounded in Self-Esteem and Trust

2. Positive Climates Enable Performance

The second discovery was that when organizations invest in positive practices that support self-esteem and trust, a number of organizational effectiveness indicators (i.e. innovation, quality, customer retention, turnover) are positively impacted. As an example, inside a single financial services company with over 40 business units, we recorded a 79.85% increase in innovation outcomes, an 18.95% increase in quality measures, an 11.63% increase in customer satisfaction, and a 6.83% decrease in employee turnover.

Looking at these findings and keeping in mind the accelerated environmental, health, and societal crisis, the circumstances have never been more perfect for a renewed set of theologies and models. We need a new, fully developed model of economic policy that can take over the dominant forces of power. This will not be a simple model, and it will be one that requires true and honest international cooperation. Our 21st-century businesses are in a unique position to lead the way and so we invite the world of business leaders to join this process of regeneration.

A NEW SET OF BEHAVIORS

Organizations are living organisms and are made up of individuals who hold a deep relationship to its collective culture. The way individuals see themselves inside an organization forms the habits of everyday practice and routine. Commonly demonstrated behaviors, meanwhile, directly shape the culture of the organization's development. In order to challenge current claims and impacts of our traditional ways of working, we must first invest in the enlargement of our taxonomies.

We cannot evaluate the trajectory of business separate from civilization and without a clear appreciation for an enlarged definition of humanity, for example. In the new world order, a business cannot be single-handedly oriented toward profit-making if we want to survive history as a species. An organization is not and cannot be a thing in itself, isolated from economics, society or culture. And individuals cannot be separated from systems they make up, and certainly cannot be pulled away from their humanities. That centering on individual and collective humanness brings relativity with a potential to drive equality and equity into the conversation that is otherwise missing at large. That centering gives us the benefit to claim that every time we single out our focus – for example, when we only go after profit; every time we disintegrate or categorize – for example, when we look down on a new or a different player; or every time we separate in class – for example, when we choose to see certain groups as fit for our culture, we are consciously or unconsciously breaking into categories and relying on theories that no longer provide predictability. It gives us permission to say when we are not actively working towards unity under a set of agreed-upon foundational values that honor everyone equally, when we operate without trust and from an economical model that struggles to provide for all, that we are, indeed, dis-serving our core purpose and becoming blind-sided to possibilities. On the other hand, when we can integrate, include, and innovate together, we become able to contribute to the creation of many more prosperous opportunities we may not even be able to imagine…

During our study, we discovered five common leadership behaviors that challenge the way traditional organizations conceptualize the philosophy of leading.

Behaviors

Leaders sit in many chairs
Leaders lead themselves
Leaders lead for head, heart, hand
Leaders lead for connection
Leaders lead with growth

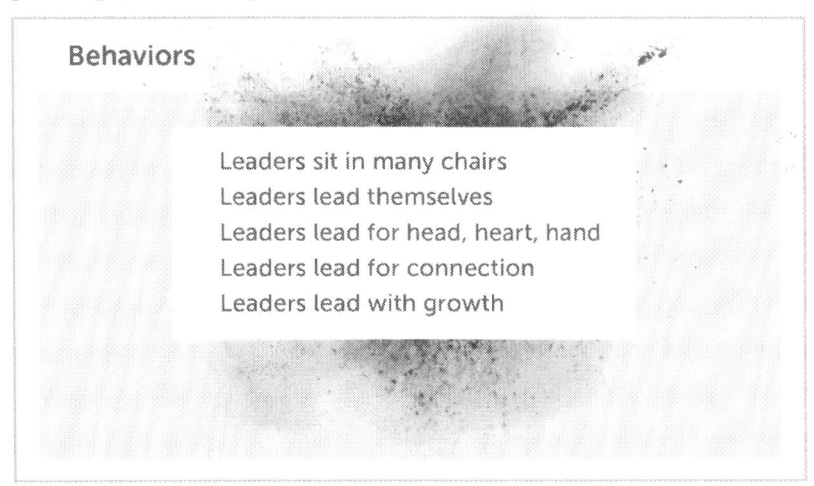

Table 7. New Behaviors for 21st-Century Leaders

Leaders Sit In Many Chairs

Inside the enduring organizations studied, there is a fundamental understanding that one's true power comes from confidence. In these organizations, we found leadership is rarely dedicated to a few at the top. Instead, all people – despite tenure, rank or title – are encouraged and supported to feel and act as an independent agent in their role or seat. People feel connected to a mission, report being engaged, trusted, and feeling empowered in their decision making. As a result, they keep a sense of responsibility and contribute to the creation of open working environments.

Twenty-first-century leadership is no longer about just power or status. Awakening humanity at work requires us to awaken potential everywhere. Given the complexity, dynamism, and diversity of the new world order, we need the full humanity, creativity, empathy, and contribution of each person in the organization to shine.

Leaders Lead Themselves

A common trait of the enduring organizations studied is a fundamental understanding that one's ability to influence a large network of peers relies heavily on their self-awareness and willingness to invest in self-improvement. There is an agreement that one's ability to nurture and grow others is deeply dependent on and supported by their own growth experiences. For this, we noted, individuals proactively seek reflections from their peers. They search and welcome new ideas for approaching perspectives, discussions, and work from a variety of angles. They take time to invest in their learning and attend activities beyond the office environment.

The new world of work is also a new world of focus, self-regulation, and presence. What we each choose not to do is often as important as what we choose to do. For instance, choosing not to blame people for errors, choosing to emphasize learning, choosing to hold off sending emails after work hours, choosing to turn off the phone and sit face-to-face for conversations, etc.

It is no longer enough just to have knowledge; it is important to also put it into practice.

Leaders Lead For Head, Heart And Hands

Another understanding we found dominant inside these organizations is the importance of authenticity to provide others with a more holistic experience.

It is a well-used phrase that leaders must win over the hearts and minds of those they hope to lead, but inside these organizations, we also found that people acknowledge that human beings are whole and complex and every day have to engage in many difficult choices about what they do and how they do it. Therefore, they often role model holistic wellbeing and look out for others at the same time.

Luckily, a variety of new studies (i.e. neuroscience) are emerging from many corners, emphasizing the connection between our brains, hearts, and bodies. In the new era, we must become aware of this connection and take accountability for the enormous impact our actions have on others' physiologies and psychologies.

Leaders Lead For Connection

In relating to their role, we found inside these organizations that people aim as much for high-quality connections as they do for high-quality operational execution. Similar to other organizations, in these companies we also found most managers report being able to climb the corporate ladder of success by getting a lot done. They, too, have implicitly developed a managerial style that emphasizes execution. The difference was that inside these organizations, people noted the longer they are treated and start to feel like "leaders", the less valuable they found this strategy to become. They developed awareness that their connections played an equal – if not more – important role in their team productivity and ultimately getting work done.

In a world where competitive advantage comes from empathy and creativity rather than technical prowess and execution excellence, it certainly looks like the best leaders in the near future will be those who lead with relationships at the center of their work.

Leaders Lead With Growth

The predominant understanding we recorded across all the organizations interviewed was their desire to continue growing. This was fascinating as everybody we spoke to mentioned their desire to leverage their authority to continually and proactively invest in skills development – both on an individual and collective level.

It is not uncommon for us to discuss "growth" in numbers inside our businesses. In a world where our global workforce is stretched in its mental and emotional capabilities, and where the pace of change is unprecedented, it becomes critical for us to redefine how we measure success and embrace an on-going learning mindset to tap and unleash potential.

Of course, it is one thing to talk about the need to develop new behaviors; it is another to learn a behavior. Especially for adults, there are a number of common issues that get in our way of learning new tricks. For one, personal (and often process) bias gets in the way. By the time we are 15, we are pretty set in the ways we learn new things[46]. Two, the learning concepts and theories we tend to leverage are completely outdated, providing little to no relevance; and finally, the ways we learn about behavior development are often missing the science behind it. We tend to think sitting in a classroom for a day or watching 2-3 minutes of video can lead to a change in behavior. In reality, information only shapes about 10% of our adult learning. The other 10% comes from inspiration and 80% of our learning happens through doing[47]. This is also why despite the amount of money poured into it – $47 billion went into corporate learning in 2018 – executive learning and development programs do not live up to their intended impact. What we need instead may be a more integrated way of learning that takes context into consideration, drives mindset shift, and provides contextual relevance for practice.

Human-centered leadership is for once not about reaching a goal, or about being perfect, nor is it about pretending to be something we are

---

46   https://opentextbc.ca/socialpsychology/chapter/biases-in-attribution/
47   https://uil.unesco.org/system/files/grale_4_final.pdf

not. It is about putting effort into being the best versions of ourselves and bringing that effort forward every day to inspire someone. We have made a lot of progress in our leadership and people practices over the years, but a lot of inconsistencies and damaging behaviors have continued. We know what is broken across our organizations. We do not need any more data or evidence. If we want to recreate, it can support us in becoming the leaders we want to be led by.

To give us all a little inspiration and to serve as a conversation starter, here are some examples of how the human-centered leadership behaviors we recorded looked compared to other organizations:

> a. Leading with self-honor and acceptance: Human-centered leadership is grounded in self-esteem that honors our holistic, humanistic experiences and drives constant energy creation and connection. It understands the importance of personal and social identity, and supports the development of self-concept inside a provided environment.
>
> The behavioral examples we recorded showed leaders paying specific attention to their attitude, valuing integration and committing to acting from a place of authenticity. For example, where a leader had childcare duty, they would leave the office at a particular time without building any specific expectations in return, like the fact they will log on in the evening and make up the time. Similarly, they would provide the necessary flexibility for their people to fulfill their personal duties as long as people remained committed to their tasks and objectives.
>
> b. Leading from a place of unconditional, compassionate love: Human-centered leadership is grounded in self-respect and unconditional love. It comprehends and honors all people's equal right to equity, dignity, and integrity. It recognizes all people for who they are, accepts their unique contribution, treats them with respect, and recognizes their value. Even in the toughest of scenarios, it leads with rational compassion to serve everyone right.

Most of the behavioral examples recorded were simple in action yet powerful in their essence, such as leaders walking around the floors on a regular basis (i.e. daily or weekly), looking people in the eye during a conversation, offering a smile without expecting one first, congratulating someone for work done well, or the simplest of them all – saying "thank you." There were also some behaviors demonstrated during more challenging scenarios. For example, showing respect for someone's emotions when having to embrace change during a restructuring announcement, or making time for self-reflection during a performance conversation.

c. Leading from a symmetry of power and equality: Human-centered leadership understands that transformation is about consciousness and transcendence is about connecting. It has self-awareness and achieves higher positive connections by being clear about yourself and others. It leads with purpose, values held, and innate strengths. It actively looks inward to stay self-connected to then be able to look outward and drive connection with others from there.

Some of the behavioral examples were leaders inquiring for participation, showing willingness to hear from everyone, listening actively to understand one's perspective, neutrality weighting options during decision-making processes, etc.

d. Leading from a practice of solitude: Human-centered leadership acknowledges the evolutionary baggage we carry around with us and continues to embrace growth as a key value despite it. It accepts our bodily limitations and honors that we are not robots. Instead, it celebrates the variance in capacities we hold that's unique for us to bring soul and magic into our work. It values the journey as much as the result.

Some of the behavioral examples recorded were grounded in more trust (of the individual and collective capability) and were driven by a leader's desire to reflect, understand, and learn from setbacks. For example, these leaders would hold reflective time after a project comes to an end. Where there was an error in the planning process, they would call for a discussion to dig deeper into possible root causes. During brainstorming, they would be satisfied with a number of possible solutions and get behind collective decisions to drive with creative energy.

As future leaders, we have to accept and own the impact we have on other people every day. When we do, our act becomes contagious. For all the leaders mentioned above in the examples, and for the ones we have been fortunate enough to serve over the years, less than a handful were not able to make progress. Furthermore, we found none of those successful leaders would consider themselves "perfect" individuals, rather, they would emphasize their willingness to learn and grow. Because the majority of the time, our circumstances do not change immediately. Rather, when we can initiate self-action and create the kind of environments where we can be ourselves and flourish as one, we can then ultimately share with others the benefits of that expanded opportunity.

A NEW SET OF MINDSETS

Our deepest assumptions and beliefs serve as guiding principles, and provide us direction and meaning in life. Our perceptions of both ourselves and others become our filters, helping us make sense of the environment, events, knowledge, past experiences, etc. As a group of scientists aware of the complexity of one's being and the range of factors that feed our behavior day to day, in the next phase of our research we challenged ourselves to discover prominent mindsets and specific attributes that acted as an enabler for the leadership behaviors described.

Mindsets[48] are a set of assumptions, views, methods, and notions we hold in understanding the world around us. In framing our lives, they serve a number of cognitive functions. For example, they inform how we make decisions, and create an incentive for us to continue, evolve,

---

48   https://www.wikiwand.com/en/Mindset

change or adopt certain ways of thinking, feeling, and acting. They are active. There is a combination of past, present, and future experiences at play in their formation. They are also dynamic and often re-iterated through our on-going interactions with the world. When the human brain processes information, we use what are known as "neural pathways." Every time our brain receives a signal, a neuron is fired and travels along a previously created pathway. But the brain cannot differentiate between what is real and what is fake. It always directs information based on what is most familiar. Therefore, if we do not exercise consciousness or stop to reflect on where to place a new piece of information, we will continuously self-validate. But there is also something known as the neuroplasticity of the brain, whereby we have a kind of secret power to send our neurons along a different pathway. This is how we can choose to learn something different. So mindsets are powered through hope and recharged through this neuroplasticity.

There is another, critical piece of information. Although the shift in behavior calls for a paradigm shift in mindsets, that paradigm shift does not usually happen overnight. It may happen in a moment; however, for most of us, it often requires our individual cognitive and affective perspective to reshape. This takes time not only because we need to learn to be mindful about the information we are receiving and create space to respond to it choicefully, but also because a transformation sometimes requires transcendence, an environmental commitment to change. This is because our ecosystem plays an equal role in changing collective behavior. You could compare it to dieters often being advised to not keep chocolate inside the home, or those trying to quit smoking to stay away from parties where people may be smoking. The same applies for an organization. While an organizational culture transformation can be predictable to a large degree, when it comes to driving new mindsets inside an organizational environment, there is a lot to address, from unconscious bias to instinct to conscious context formation.

Attributes[49], on the other hand, are a collection of qualities or characteristics that are inherent to human beings and that enable us to

---

49   https://www.ncbi.nlm.nih.gov/books/NBK64939/

overcome, enhance or diminish the manifestation of biological and psychological patterns as a result of our being. Together, this collection of beliefs and qualities orient our reactions and day-to-day tendencies. At any given time, they present us with a choice, empower us, and equip us.

In understanding the key theologies that enabled the kind of leadership behaviors described above, in the next phase of our research, we searched for a common thread across day-to-day behaviors. To our surprise, we were able to record a number of new mindsets that are not often precedent in our current work environments.

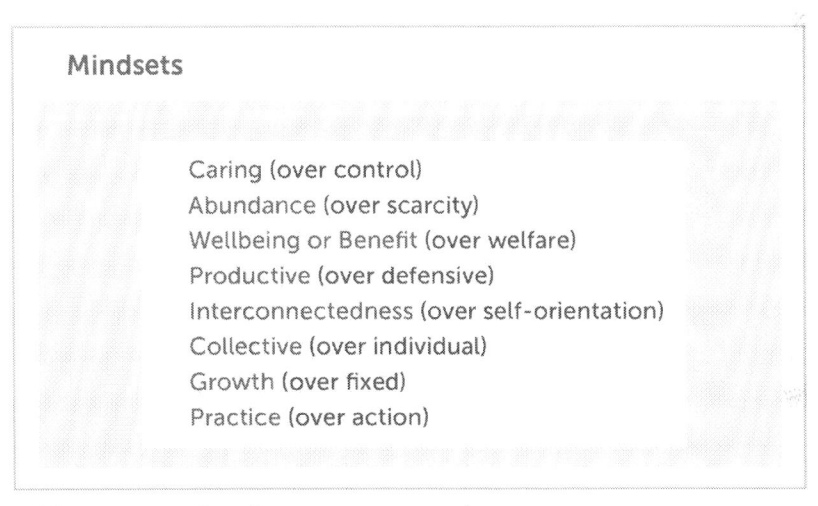

Mindsets

Caring (over control)
Abundance (over scarcity)
Wellbeing or Benefit (over welfare)
Productive (over defensive)
Interconnectedness (over self-orientation)
Collective (over individual)
Growth (over fixed)
Practice (over action)

Table 8. New Mindsets for 21st-Century Leaders

Caring (Over Control)

Our experiences at work and in life generally are defined by "micro moments." These are single moments of connection we make in a given environment and they can come in the form of eye contact, a smile or simply by being present. In studying enduring organizations, we found one emotion common in these micro moments: One's sense of caring.

Caring is the degree of affection and compassion people feel and express toward one another.

There are great benefits to carrying a caring mindset inside a work environment. With a caring mindset, workers experience lower absenteeism, less burnout, greater teamwork, and higher job satisfaction[50]. Because of its measurable value, companies such as PepsiCo, Southwest Airlines, Whole Foods Market, The Container Store, and Zappos have begun to explicitly include caring in their leadership principles.

What makes caring possible for organizations is a concept called "virtuousness." Virtuousness is best associated with what individuals and organizations aspire to be when they are at their best. This mindset enables individuals to carry a sense of naivety towards all things they come into contact with, serving as a moral compass in seeing and meeting others at the level of their humanity. Interestingly, though, as leaders of our organizations, many of us struggle with "self-righteousness." We lack the qualities necessary to show humility, and struggle to say, "I don't know", "Tell me", "I want to learn" or "I missed that, help me understand it better, please!" Not only is our ignorance often invisible to ourselves, we often do not know how to show it and/or we are hugely uncomfortable demonstrating vulnerability. Instead of trying to overcome the inner critique available to us, we often end up giving in, which results in the generation of a self-perception usually based on fear and judgment. This pattern pulls us back during discussions and prevents us from coming forth and saying, "I have never had that experience, help me understand it."

The opposite of caring is control. This is the degree of perceived regulation inside a given environment. These are the kinds of environments that are mostly comprised of conscious and unconscious policies and procedures. When we carry a mindset of control, we tend to avoid emotions inside the environment. There is no room for us or others to express our emotions. When we stay in this state for prolonged periods of time, our stress hormones get triggered and eventually we become even more fearful and resistant of change than before.

---

50   https://hbr.org/2019/11/making-work-less-stressful-and-more-engaging-for-your-employees

Unfortunately, this is also the state that can sometimes manifest itself as actions of emotional abuse in power[51].

In a caring mindset, however, we see value-based positive behaviors. Because we can give ourselves the permission to remain connected to our emotions, we grow a perception that there is enough space to be authentic. This causes our brains to release positive neurotransmitters that expand our ability to gain and offer more emotional connection. As a result, we become even more open and can better engage with our surroundings.

Abundance (Over Scarcity)

The kind of living capitalist system we have built in the past two hundred or so years relies on our constant work for economic independence and attainment. This way of approaching the world has trained us to focus on scarcity as a default mode.

A *scarcity* mindset focuses on what is lacking – all the time. The word "scarce" comes from the old French word "scars", meaning "restricted in quantity." In this mindset, we perceive everything to be limited – time, money, love. We have the ultimate lenses for "zero-sum" thinking, that for me to gain, something or someone has to give... As a result, we find ourselves consciously or unconsciously concerned about what can go wrong most of the time. This is also true of work environments. Leaders who allow a scarcity mindset into their culture pay a high price[52]. When resources (compensation, opportunity, recognition) are perceived to be limited, paranoia, fear, and politics thrive. People become nervous of their future and afraid to make a mistake. As a result, teamwork and innovation suffer.

What is interesting about the organizations we studied is that people understand the impact of having a limited view on life, and instead, work from a perspective of efficacy and abundance. Abundance is

---

51 https://www.ncbi.nlm.nih.gov/pmc/articles/PMC4768593/

52 https://www.amazon.com/gp/product/1599951681/ref=as_li_tl?ie=UTF8&camp=1789&creative=9325&creativeASIN=1599951681&linkCode=as2&tag=wwwdrjuliec0d-20&linkId=9a8cd405af209e07fea90f758c004ec7

a wealth of something. An *abundant* mindset feeds into our confidence because we know there is enough in the environment to be able to spend it on things that matter to us most. This mindset enables individuals to carry a sense of on-going responsibility and supports development of individual and collective confidence to better take in, process, and utilize information and other resources. Leaders with an abundant mindset broaden their perspective to integrate needs, timetables, and experiences to allocate resources more wisely[53]. In return, employees find the necessary space and sources to connect to their purpose, creative thinking, and stakeholder management. In other words, inside such environments, individuals are free of future anxiety. Therefore, they can better coordinate aspirations and collaborate on action, which results in the creation of higher meaning. As a result, organizations focus on opportunity and synergy creation and become more profitable[54].

Wellbeing Or Benefit (Over Welfare)

Similar to carrying a "zero-sum" focus as described above, we have, for years, leveraged leadership and management practices that were originally designed to serve utility maximization. Many organizations are still investing millions of dollars into benefit programs, which is often supporting one's individual welfare. But *welfare* is not the same as having environmental, cognitive, social or affective wellbeing, and focusing on welfare alone is not sufficient to raise equity with our employees. In fact, science shows us that welfare is recorded as only one of the conditions necessary to drive equitable total compensation[55].

---

[53] https://www.orellfuessli.ch/shop/home/artikeldetails/ID147735512.html?ProvID=10917737&gclid=Cj0KCQjwrsGCBhD1ARIsALILBYp3d5jBWYJ9z1UhozjBmgCWa9Q-LAp8mqH4FhSRW2dZmCvUF6uZm4saAn1JEALw_wcB

[54] https://www.orellfuessli.ch/shop/home/artikeldetails/ID147735512.html?ProvID=10917737&gclid=Cj0KCQjwrsGCBhD1ARIsALILBYp3d5jBWYJ9z1UhozjBmgCWa9Q-LAp8mqH4FhSRW2dZmCvUF6uZm4saAn1JEALw_wcB

[55] https://courses.lumenlearning.com/wm-principlesofmanagement/chapter/employee-compensation-incentive-and-benefits-strategies/

Indeed, while working with global organizations, we often come across many professionals who are justly compensated for their work and yet at the same time, are incredibly depleted when it comes to inner resources. So, what might the missing link be here? It is our attention to wellbeing.

Wellbeing is about one's holistic resourcefulness. A wellbeing mindset considers all aspects of a humanly experience such as one's attitudes, behaviors, emotional capacity as well as capability set and skills. It pays equal attention to work design, environment, connections, and development to ignite internal motivation in addition to considering external motivators. Having a wellbeing mindset can help prevent health problems and contribute to formation of positive work experiences, and it is equally good for organizations. When a leader acknowledges all aspects required for someone to thrive, they become relationally more attentive towards everyone's unique needs. Research validates that this focus indeed drives better inclusion and a feeling of equity amongst peers[56].

If you are wondering how to make the perspective shift, it is important to realize that when people value "integration", on both an individual and collective level, as part of their development, it supports their ability to approach things more authentically and work towards forming healthy relationships as a consequence of their wellbeing. This not only increases relatedness, it also supports a sense of belonging inside organizations. In other words, wellbeing is not only a core responsibility and a critical performance strategy for businesses. The more we become focused on holistic offerings, the more possibilities we create for equitable earning and belonging.

Productive (Over Defensive)

As leaders, it is tempting for us to create a world in which we are perfect. We can choose partners, friends, hire people who make us feel faultless at all times. We can always pretend to have the answers. The

---

[56] https://www.ccl.org/articles/leading-effectively-articles/5-powerful-ways-to-take-real-action-on-dei-diversity-equity-inclusion/

question, however, is then how would we find constructive criticism that can support our growth? It is an unfortunate fact that in the current environment of constant competition, we find many defensive routines inside organizations.

In a *defensive* mindset, individuals or groups only seek out information that protects them because a defensive mindset is by nature self-protective and self-deceptive. When people become victims of such interpersonal interactions, it creates a need for them to close up and protect themselves from embarrassment and threat. Truth can be shut out when it is seen as threatening, and decisions may be made on false assumptions[57]. As a result, this sort of behavior vastly shrinks individual and collective performance.

A *productive* mindset, on the other hand, creates opportunities for reasoning. It provides a neutral base for informed and transparent decision making. It actively seeks out valid knowledge that is testable and provides constructive data to help others achieve better results through collective brainstorming. This, in return, vastly increases an organization's focus on result-achieving.

Inside the surveyed organizations, people hold a level of self-esteem that supports them to rely on a mechanism where information flows both ways in a mutually respective way so that both parties can flourish. This sort of confidence then enables individuals to keep a future-focused and shared reality, and motivates better allocation of resources for solution-building.

Interconnectedness (Over Self-orientation)

Interconnectedness refers to the state of being joined together. Despite the common belief that our bodies function independently and as individuals, our brains and bodies actually work like distributed networks – no part acts without the other and our cells are closely connected. Similarly, we discover there is interconnectedness to our human condition. Neuroscience shows us[58] that when we feel

---

57   https://link.springer.com/content/pdf/10.3758/BF03197497.pdf
58   https://www.ncbi.nlm.nih.gov/pmc/articles/PMC3874845/

disconnected from others or our surroundings, our wellbeing gets negatively impacted. We end up having higher inflammation at the cellular level, and emotionally we become more susceptible to sadness, anxiety, and depression. In the workplace, we depend on team members for a sense of belonging, and our organizations depend on a network of global minds and a number of product/service opportunities to drive value.

When we feel connected to one another, not only do we become healthier, our consciousness expands in ways we cannot imagine. For example, we become better able to engage in:

- synthesis, an ability to combine information to create something new,

- emergence, an ability to detect an outcome of marrying factors together, and,

- causality, an ability to find feedback loops and gain deeper perspective in agency.

Inside the organizations interviewed, we found people valued altruism and acted in ways that were more benevolent. This mindset provides then a grounding on diversity of thought and raises the interest and possibility of connections over self-making[59].

Collective (Over Individual)

The concept of a collective mindset has been a long-standing one in sociology; however, we use it here to describe how information is mapped and shared inside a specific network. Driven by our traditional hierarchical structures inside organizations, we often find information being dedicated to a single individual and/or being shared from one source.

A *collective* mindset is one that focuses on mutual accountability and result sharing. It considers relationships between parts and wholes, stability and change, rationality and creativity rather than

---

59   https://books.google.ch/books?id=YePSyMfjqb8C&printsec=frontcover&source=gbs_atb&redir_esc=y#v=onepage&q&f=false

the boundaries that divide groups, ideas, and spaces. It harnesses diversity by welcoming differences, treating apparent opposites as interdependent, drawing evidence by multiple ways of understanding. As a result, leaders with a collective mindset provide a home for differences, celebrating both individuality and mutuality, welcoming cohesion amongst peers.

We discovered that, within these organizations, people carry an institutional view into information collection, processing, and sharing. They work to get eyes on a single goal, shared measures, engage in mutually reinforcing activities, communicate proactively, etc. to build trust and adapt collective ways of working. This mindset[60] enables individuals to contribute equally to group goals, share information more transparently, document, and support various activities over a single, dedicated task.

On-going Learning (Over Fixed)

A *growth* mindset is the belief that our basic abilities can be developed and improved through dedication and effort. When we have a growth mindset, we lean into the required effort to grow our potential in the ways we want it to in life. For example, in her studies, Dr. Carol Dweck discovered that when students believe they can get smarter, they understand that effort makes them stronger. As a result, they put in extra time and effort, and that leads to higher achievement[61].

A fixed mindset, on the other hand, is the belief that our abilities are predefined and cannot be changed. When we have a fixed mindset, we tend to shy away[62] from challenges because we do not want to feel embarrassed or humiliated in front of others. This can be problematic as our fear of making mistakes[63] can lead us to avoid challenges and

---

60 http://www.scielo.br/pdf/rsocp/v22n52/02.pdf
61 https://www.indiebound.org/book/9780345472328
62 https://www.psychologytoday.com/us/basics/shyness
63 https://www.psychologytoday.com/us/blog/click-here-happiness/201804/three-ways-overcome-fear-failure

new experiences that could help us grow and unleash our potential with others.

On the other hand, a growth mindset can help us focus on the opportunities ahead and discover more joy in the process because we know we value learning and discovery over what others may think of us. Neuroscience now shows us the great benefits of a growth mindset. With this mindset, our muscles relax, we breathe better, and our internal energy reserves expand vastly[64]. But there are also organizational benefits. Because our energy radiates contagiously, when we approach possibilities with an open mind, we become more collaborative and our collective resilience grows over time[65].

When we develop a desire for on-going learning, it supports the process of discovery and injects hope inside people's hearts towards a possibility of growth[66]. Inside the organizations we studied, we found people gave more of an ear to their "inner champions" vs. their "inner critiques." This in return made them realize that, though they may not have control over life events, they do hold the responsibility and accountability for their decision making.

Practice (Over Action)

In today's business environment, many organizations have become obsessed with action-taking in the workplace. Granted, balancing long- and short-term impact can be a real struggle for today's leaders, but when we value action over impact, we often end up with an overwhelming list of things to do and sometimes lose sight of our key purpose.

"Reflect" in Latin means "to refold", which refers to turning our attention inwards. A *reflective* mindset is one that allows us to be thoughtful, examine familiar experiences in a new light, and set the stage for developing innovative ideas. There are two ways of reflecting on an experience: reflection-in-action and reflection-on-action.

---

64   https://www.ncbi.nlm.nih.gov/pmc/articles/PMC5836039/
65   https://files.eric.ed.gov/fulltext/EJ1169801.pdf
66   https://www.mindsetworks.com/science/

Reflection-in-action is being in a sequence of thoughts while we are performing a task.

Reflection-on-action is the process of reconstruction after the task is concluded in reach of drawing lessons from that experience. Research shows us that this is a better approach for achieving sustainable business development results. This is primarily related to the way we learn as adults. Unlike children, we learn best through experimentation. By choosing a suitable reflective moment, we create an opportunity to remind ourselves of a past or similar experience, we consider the future as well as the expectations of others, and only afterwards do we apply learning into current practice. Otherwise, we become exposed to relying on mental patterns and often end up conforming to individual and process bias.

Inside the organizations we studied, we discovered people prefer a "reflective practice[67]" over being in constant action. This mindset puts emphasis on consistency in time over immediate action and short-term results, and engages people in the process of learning.

IS IT POSSIBLE TO SHIFT A MINDSET?

The shift in a mindset is surely a powerful way to ignite sustainable change which can serve as an enabler for individual growth and to unleash new possibilities inside an organization. Often people wait for others to change, but understanding that change can begin just as well with one person may provide a higher sense of responsibility for us as individuals, that we can be that one individual to get change started. Through raised consciousness and increased self-awareness, we can contribute to macro shifts in organizational norms. Sometimes a small shift[68] in context or interference is all it takes to shift from cognitive to affective perspective-taking. That said, a mindset change is not easy. It is not about picking up a few pointers; it is rather about seeing the world in a new way.

---

67   https://www.wikiwand.com/en/Reflective_practice
68   https://www.ncbi.nlm.nih.gov/pmc/articles/PMC6026651/

We all carry positive and negatively charged mindsets. Let us note the importance of this, as the biodiversity of our thoughts, emotions, and behavior patterns provide us with a survival instinct. The key is in growing our consciousness, and recognizing that specific triggers can really help us expand our potential into the future. Notice, for example, what happens when you encounter someone who is better than you in an area you pride yourself on? What thoughts go through your mind when you feel threatened? Reflect on why you think you end up there and how you may be reflecting that state in your leadership style. This sort of insight will give you the power to label those personas and the necessary will to overcome some stories that may be working against you. Once you untangle those knots, you will grow capacity to better handle complex and complicated situations as leaders.

Whether officially recognized as a leader or not, we each play a key role in our workplaces and societies. In the ways that we are, that we relate to and work with each other, we get to shape each other's day-to-day experiences. Every day, we are faced with a situation in which we have the option to be the smartest in the room or create an environment where everyone else is. We can be present without blocking others. We can share what we hold inside our minds, hearts, and souls without trying to prove or disprove. We can engage to meet the conditions of a full heart, but only with an empathic ear; we can ask beautiful questions to help design beautiful experiences. When we lean in, our capacity expands. When our capacity expands, we become able to change someone else's world. When we touch lives, our act becomes contagious.

The key to being, of course, remains in our intent.

PART 3

CORE HUMAN ATTRIBUTES

The first time I discovered the power of intent inside of me I was 10 years old. I had just enrolled in a private middle school as a scholarship student and discovered I was the youngest in my class, which would prove to be a pattern in my years to follow in life.

I learned that week that there was an aerobics class open to students of a certain age. I remember staying after school hours, watching the others practice and being mesmerized. I remember finding immense joy in the music and wanting to dance while standing there, outside. There was an energy that carried me away, and my eyes were dazzled by the sight of all those sparkly uniforms. I wanted in. Eventually, I convinced my mother to persuade the teacher, who finally conceded to let me stand at the back and learn from the others, offering no promise of membership to the team.

The first day I showed up to class, I took a shine to Demet. She was the teacher of the aerobics class. She was young and beautiful. She had a smile that lit up the whole room. She sang, danced, joked vividly with students, always teaching them new tricks and challenging them; pushing their abilities to the limit. It was impossible not to be inspired by her.

When it came to Christmas that year, the school had planned a Secret Santa. I remember sitting up night after night, praying that I would be the one to draw Demet's name. I wanted her to "see" me, to "hear" me, and to "care" for me. It wasn't a romantic infatuation, rather an intense desire to become one of the best students my school had ever seen.

When the day came for the names to be drawn, I pulled a different name from the bag. I remember being very confused. I had a sense of certainty that I was going to draw Demet's name. How could this be? That night, when my mother returned home from work, I was exhausted and half asleep on the couch from all the crying. She said, "Hey! I heard there was a mix-up with the name drawing today. I guess it will be redone at school tomorrow, did you hear?"

I knew it. I knew it right there and then; my faith had returned.

The next morning, I rushed to school and waited impatiently for the end of class. When it was time to redraw, I patiently waited for it to be my turn. And then, I dug my hand into the hat and proudly drew out a piece of white paper that read "Demet."

POWER OF INTENTION

An *intention* is most frequently defined as a directive thought to perform a determined action. It is considered a mental state that represents a psychological commitment towards carrying out an action. Because of this, it is a common belief that intention involves pre-planning in the brain, some foresight in the heart, and perhaps some bodily preparation. As a result, those thoughts targeted to an end can affect the parts of an outcome they bring about[69]. In this traditional view, an intention is described as a relatively abstract representation that has a causal effect on our behaviors. This basic understanding is widely employed in the philosophy, psychology, and neuroscience of intention[70] (Davidson, 1978; Bratman, 1999; Haggard and Libet, 2001), and is equally supported by those who have developed critical views on the actual causal effectiveness of such states of intention[71] (Gollwitzer, 1999; Holton, 1999, 2003; Gollwitzer and Sheeran, 2006).

There is another way of looking at intention. That the concepts of concentration and intensity are brought forward as key descriptors of an

---

69 https://pubmed.ncbi.nlm.nih.gov/19245175/

70 https://www.frontiersin.org/articles/10.3389/fpsyg.2019.00946/full#ref22

71 https://www.frontiersin.org/articles/10.3389/fpsyg.2019.00946/full#ref30

intention and intention is seen as an all-encompassing act, meaning it has control over our life experiences. In her 2007 book, *The Intention Experiment*, author Lynne McTaggart uses research conducted across a number of universities – Princeton, MIT, Stanford – to showcase and reveal that intent is capable of affecting all aspects of our lives. Similarly, William A. Tiller, a now-retired professor of Stanford University, argues "For the last 400 years, an unstated assumption of science is that human intention cannot affect what we call physical reality. Our experimental research of the past decade shows that, for today's world and under the right conditions, this assumption is no longer correct."

It does not matter which definition you feel closer to, it is a fact that intention has some level of power over us. It is therefore a pity that understanding and communicating with intent has not been of much importance in the world of business over the past several decades. Vision documents are often created and then filed away, revisited from time to time when a change needs to be communicated. Only a handful of leaders are expected to contribute to the evolution and execution of that vision. Nowadays and certainly with the support of neuroscience, there is more research around the power of storytelling[72], and organizations are finally starting to pay more attention to the value of intent and how it should be spread across a number of audiences and geographies, shaping both individual and collective behavior.

The power of intention is most closely related to the *clarity* in purpose, attention and conscientiousness we can bring to our development, key associations, and beyond. We find an intention predominantly comes to life in spacious moments, disconnected from time, and it seems to demonstrate a connection to an eternal creative source beyond our comprehension, proving influence over the way we view our individual and collective experiences of the past, the present, and the future. An intention is both impactful in terms of its storyline and the outcomes of its effect, and at the same time, it cannot be separated from the process of behavior development it supports. Imagine, for example, someone acting generously towards another – a behavior that can be observed and that looks positive on the surface... How

---

72   https://www.ncbi.nlm.nih.gov/pmc/articles/PMC4445577/

are we – as the observer – to rationalize the motive without having a clear understanding of the person's past experience, their current relationship to the other person, the environmental circumstances, and/or without having factual knowledge of their intention?

Human behavior is extremely complex and highly influenced by social interactions. This is why most of our behaviors remain unpredictable day to day. No matter how much we think we know about someone or how much we think we can predict their actions, we can never be sure of their stories, intrinsic motives or final behaviors. In fact, some of the time, people may not even recognize their own storyline or intentions. This only becomes more true inside multi-faceted environments like global corporations. While our individual experiences shape the behaviors of the collective in forming a system, once we become part of a system, our individual experiences get impacted tremendously by the dominant collective behaviors.

There is one thing, however, that we know and can rely on. It is that the intention[73] we put into achieving a certain outcome supports not only the formation, but also the performance of the behavior carrying us into the outcome. In looking to understand the different evolutionary patterns inside the organizations we studied, and in search of specific *attributes* – the quality of characteristics that may be in support of our behavior development, as described earlier – we were able to validate that where an individual, consciously or unconsciously, chooses to place their intention and leans into the given attributes available, has a differentiated impact on their individual behavior formation as well as the climate. Where we, as individual leaders, choose to play when it comes to qualities available to us, actually enhances or diminishes the outcome of our and others' potential experience.

This is an important finding as, once again, we – as leaders of the new world order – are presented with the choice of who we want to become and the kind of environments we aspire to build for the benefit of those we lead.

---

73   https://www.researchgate.net/publication/325972981_Exploring_the_Link_between_Intention_and_Behavior_in_Consumer_Research

THE EIGHT CORE HUMAN ATTRIBUTES

The eight core human attributes, which we identify as the genetic code of any human being, are: Purpose, courage, foresight, emotional insight, wonder, wisdom, compassion, and mastery.

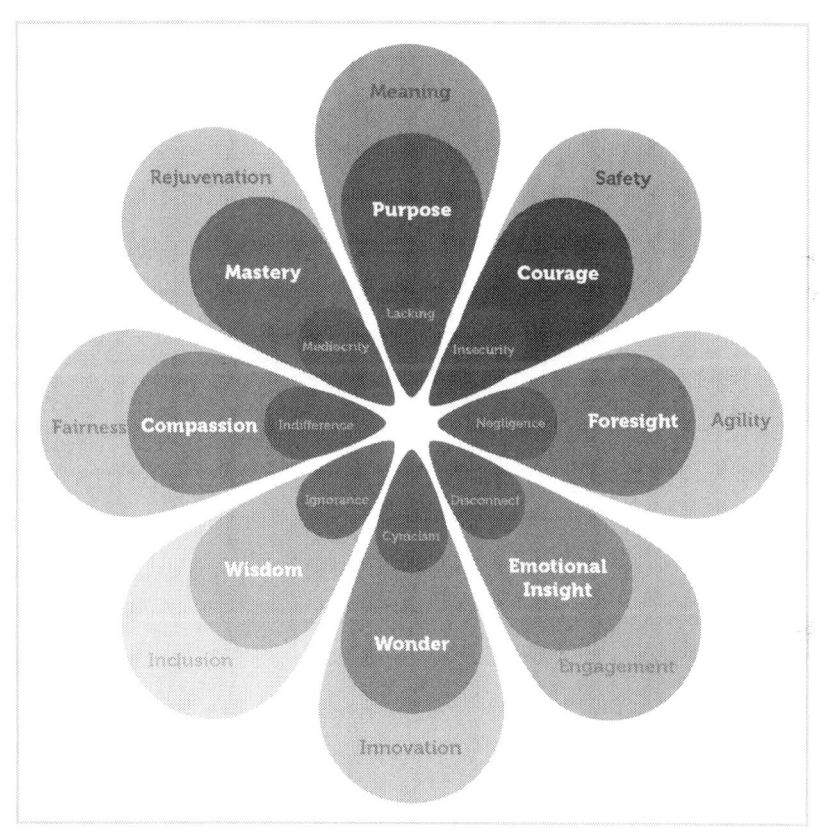

Table 9. Core Attributes of Human-Centered Leadership

It is critical to highlight that all of these attributes are innate to all human beings, regardless of geography, income, education or experience. Each one of us is born with these unique qualities. Though there is a natural order to the attributes in evolutionary development terms; we have come to recognize them as non-linear. Furthermore, they are strongly tied to one's self-esteem and self-reflection in terms of their ability to grow, expand or shrink in capacity. Choosing to exercise one – whether on its bright or shadow side – has a significant effect on our own personal behavioral development, but also a knock-on effect on the formation of the cultures we are part of. The kind of leadership behaviors we present as a consequence of our capacities would in return cause a number of positive or negative outcomes that can enhance or diminish the organizations we lead.

We believe that understanding these attributes in full will support future leaders in enhancing their self-awareness and will equip them with the practical tools they need to build desirable and sustainable working environments more intently.

PURPOSE

A purpose is a core belief or an aspiration as to why we do what we do or why we exist in the first place. It is often thought of as an understanding of the WHY of a behavior or a situation and/or a specific mission in service of something greater.

Purpose is also frequently defined as a central, self-organizing life aim on an individual level. It is known to be the greatest source of meaning, which is often referred to by academics and philosophers as a path to the good life. The kind of meaning underlined here is most commonly understood by the concept of *eudaimonia,* an ancient Greek word for "human flourishing."

Psychologists who study meaning-formation[74] have pointed to three important anchors that define purpose:

1. Core aims and aspirations of what we want to do and who we want to be,

2. Coherence or making sense of life and weaving threads together,

3. Significance beyond the trivial or momentary – orienting toward a bigger value.

Empirical research[75] shows us that without clear purpose, goals or values, we experience a considerable amount of stress, struggling to reach meaning formation.

74   https://www.wikiwand.com/en/Meaning-making
75   https://www.researchgate.net/publication/297579628_Existential_Psychotherapy

Inside our human bodies, our hearts and blood vessels are not technically components of our nervous systems, but, our brains and central nervous systems are linked closely to our cardiovascular function. In other words, the activity of your heart is intimately monitored and regulated by your brain. For example, your heart races when you feel nervous, anxious or excited. In experiencing such emotions, our brain initiates a series of events that lead to the secretion of adrenaline, causing the heart to beat even faster. This is a loop[76] that will diminish our physical resources and when prolonged, have a lasting impact on our stress levels.

When we have a clear sense of purpose, we are presented by the possibility of not only realizing who we are (psychological impact), which leads to us feeling more authenticity (spiritual impact), but we also experience better synchronization between our hearts and brains, preserving our most sacred natural resource (our brain; the mental impact), and decreasing emotional stress and anxiety (physical impact). In that process, purpose is important to us as individuals because it points us towards the possibility of self-expression, providing opportunity for us to bring who we are, our natural strengths, and what we want from our life and from our work into the conversation.

Most of us experience checking in and out of purpose over a lifetime. For example, do you recall a time when you asked yourself why you were here on Earth and what you were living for? Or do you recall a time when you were doing work and did not realize where the time had gone? Both of these are purpose!

All of us at some point in our journeys find ourselves asking existential questions that are often inspired by our deepest thoughts, aspirations, and experiences. At times, we struggle to connect to our core purpose, our life mission, and to find meaning. Because of this, it is fair to say that purpose is simultaneously one of the best and least known phenomena in life. The lack of awareness and understanding of it results in chaos, miscommunication, dysfunction, and the formation of unproductive communities. The dominance of it may be felt in value-conflicting situations causing individual suf-

---

76   https://www.ncbi.nlm.nih.gov/pmc/articles/PMC4564234/

fering when one does not have enough emotional agility to navigate through it. Purpose also tends to evolve with the situation you find yourself in over time[77].

Purpose In The World Of Business

In the world of business, purpose is both a hot topic and an unsolved dilemma. Corporations with a lack of strategic purpose fail to engage stakeholders fully while individual employees struggle to find inspiration and motivation.

According to BrightHouse and Boston Consulting Group's 2017 analysis[78], in organizations that achieved a high score for purpose, there are more than twice as many Total Shareholder Return (TSR) performers as an organization with low performers.

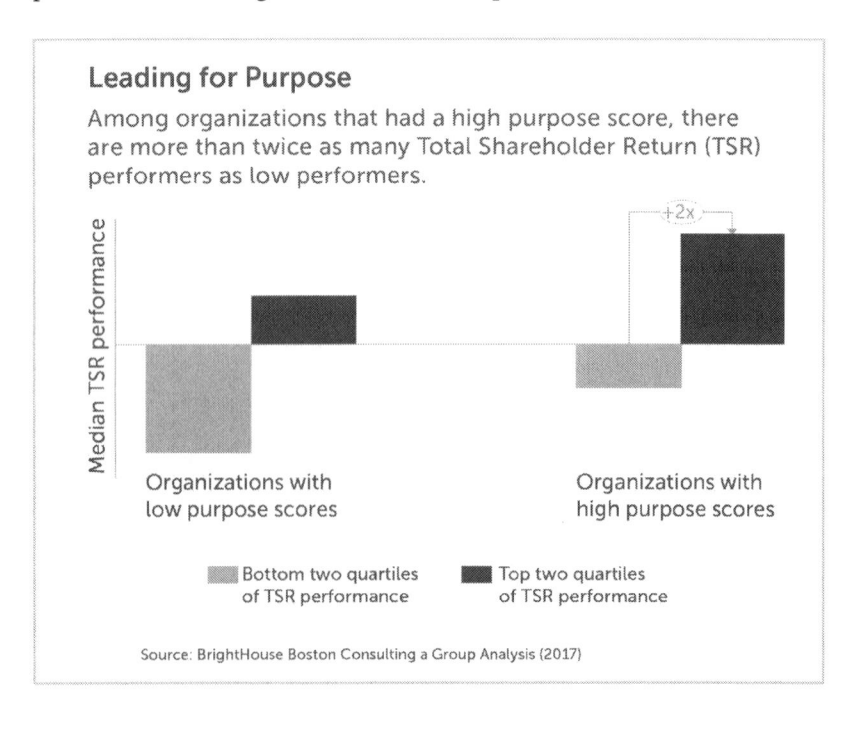

Leading for Purpose

Among organizations that had a high purpose score, there are more than twice as many Total Shareholder Return (TSR) performers as low performers.

Organizations with low purpose scores

Organizations with high purpose scores

Bottom two quartiles of TSR performance

Top two quartiles of TSR performance

Source: BrightHouse Boston Consulting a Group Analysis (2017)

---

77 https://opentextbc.ca/socialpsychology/chapter/the-social-self-the-role-of-the-social-situation/

78 https://www.bcg.com/en-ch/publications/2017/transformation-behavior-culture-purpose-power-transform-organization.aspx

Similarly, Paul Zak in his study of neuroscience of narratives[79] found that strategic narratives embodying purpose make us pay better attention and create the emotion needed to inspire us to act. Scholars studying ideological messages[80] found that organizations play an important role in shaping or influencing the meaning of work for their employees.

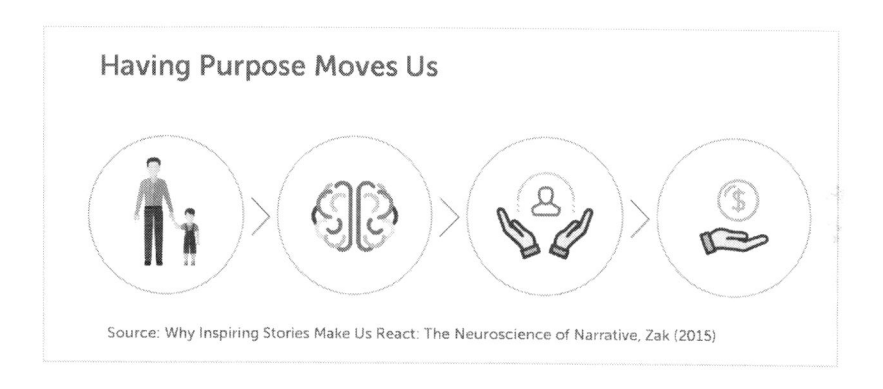

Having Purpose Moves Us

Source: Why Inspiring Stories Make Us React: The Neuroscience of Narrative, Zak (2015)

Researchers have also explored how certain leadership styles can influence the degree to which work is perceived as meaningful. This research[81] particularly emphasizes the meaningfulness-related outcomes of transformational leadership, defined as going "beyond exchanging inducements for desired performance by developing, intellectually stimulating, and inspiring followers to transcend their own self-interests for a higher collective purpose, mission, or vision" (Howell & Avolio, 1993, p. 891). Furthermore, organizations and the symbolism of its leaders' interpretations of, communications about, and responses to various work events and circumstances therefore have an important influence on the meaning people place on their work (Podolny et al., 2005).

---

79   https://www.ncbi.nlm.nih.gov/pmc/articles/PMC4445577/
80   https://faculty.wharton.upenn.edu/wp-content/uploads/2013/04/Grant Hofmann_OBHDP2011.pdf
81   https://www.researchgate.net/publication/228857668_Transformational_Leadership_and_Job_Behaviors_The_Mediating_Role_of_Core_Job_Characteristics

The self-determination theory (SDT)[82], which represents a broad framework for the study of human motivation and personality, explains that the conditions supporting one's experience are grounded in our need to (1) serve self, (2) grow competence, and (3) build relatedness. These are the motivators that foster the most willful and high-quality forms of motivation and engagement for workplace activities including enhanced performance, persistence, and creativity.

Leaders can inspire work with meaningfulness by prompting employees to go beyond their personal needs or goals in favor of those tied to a broader mission or purpose. In fact, the motivators from SDT have been translated into workplace language as autonomy, mastery, and purpose. Depending on the degree to which these three psychological needs are supported or unsupported within a social context has been proven to drive a robust detrimental impact on wellness, both in and of that setting[83]. In other words, purpose is not only important for our organizations because it helps mobilize forces; it is also important because it helps us protect the wellbeing of our most important asset – people.

Purpose In The Fortune 500 Organizations

In all the organizations we studied, where resilience levels were high and stress levels were low, individuals were (1) clear on their life's purpose the majority of time and (2) could connect this to the company mission.

Through our research, we were able to validate that purpose is not only a philosophical concept, rather establishing and pursuing a sense of purpose in life has a proven bearing on our health and wellbeing.

Furthermore, we were able to validate that in environments where leaders were reportedly connected to a purpose – meaning leaders

---

82   https://www.wikiwand.com/en/Self-determination_theory#:~:text=Self%2Ddetermination%20theory%20(SDT),without%20external%20influence%20and%20interference.

83   https://selfdeterminationtheory.org/theory/

knew about their personal life mission, could put it to use effectively through their role, and could connect it to their leadership mission and to the company vision – they were able to narrate inspiring stories to drive employees towards a specific mission. As a result, organizations experienced better meaning formation as a whole.

Similarly, we found the opposite to be true when it came to lack of purpose. Inside environments where leaders were reported to be lacking a clear purpose – either because they did not know or understand it, or they could not connect it to their life mission – leaders struggled to bring organizational missions to life. These leaders were unable to consistently narrate stories to inspire their employees. As a result, organizations had a harder time experiencing inspiration and meaning formation as a whole.

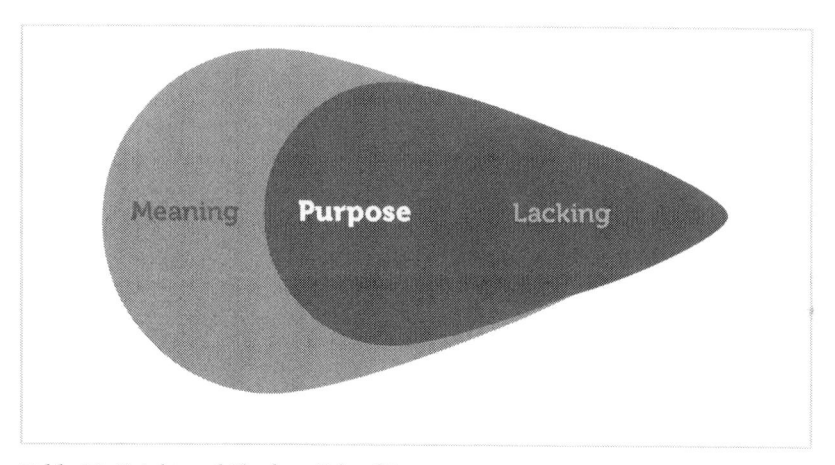

Table 10. Bright and Shadow Side of Purpose

Time To Invest In Purpose

It is time we acknowledge that purpose is a fundamental human need. The level of connection we perceive to have to a given purpose has profound consequences for how we become who we are, how we experience life, and how we relate to people, as well as how far we lean in, how much we accomplish, and the level of our work performance.

The way purpose is self-organizing[84] provides a framework for systematic behavior patterns we present in everyday life. From a practical perspective, purpose embodies and awakens an intrinsic motivation while providing a reason for our being and belonging. By connecting to a given purpose, then, we find ourselves presented with a choice in the moment to develop attachment to a growing idea and/or to develop engagement with a mission or a target effort. Through that self-organization we develop inner connections to a mission, a task, an effort towards goal setting, and a desire in allocating necessary resources.

This connection to a purpose also better equips us to cope with the curveballs that are thrown our way because our desire to make sense of the environment helps us rationalize our core mission. As a result, we often become quicker to pick ourselves up after a fall and/or manage our capacity more effectively. In that sense, purpose supports us to better experience meaning in a sustained fashion.

At an organizational level, when an employee experiences meaning at work, they are more engaged, more committed, and more aligned to the organization's values and/or goals. Often this connection leads to increased performance and productivity.

In a way, it is a shame that our current educational systems do not teach us how to find our life missions. That said, if you are going to do one thing for yourself and your organization today, let that be investing in finding your purpose, connecting to it, and leading from it. Remember that not being able to find it, or being disconnected from it, only produces confusion, frustration, and biased decision making – both on an individual and organizational level.

COURAGE

The word "courage" comes from the Old French "corage" and from the Latin word "cor" meaning the heart. Think of it this way: If purpose is about understanding what drives us, courage is about staying

---

84   https://www.jstor.org/stable/2635068

true to the purpose in the heart. Now, this is as tricky, if not more so than connecting to purpose.

Courage is most often recognized as the absence of fear or discomfort. Imagine someone filing their nails in a public place or someone walking rather quickly behind you on a dark night. How about watching violence on TV? Does it trigger any sense of irritation, fear or a shiver perhaps? There is no doubt that we can all picture events that trigger physiological reactions in us and make our hairs stand on end! Demonstrating courage is about taking action despite the feeling of fear or discomfort we may experience in our bodies.

Human feelings and thoughts – though they originate in the brain – have a strong connection to our bodies. Philosophers have argued this for thousands of years and now neuroscience shows us that emotions and thoughts infuse both the mind and the body. For example, while thinking negative thoughts or feeling negative emotions can often raise our blood pressure, thinking positive thoughts and feeling positive emotions can often strengthen our immune systems. Whether we remain conscious of this fact or not, our minds and emotions are "embodied" and have an impact on how we behave.

In scientific terms, courage is best related[85] to our willingness to be vulnerable in the face of uncertainty, risk, and emotional exposure. It is defined as an intention engaging us in something that may involve risk while in search of a noble or a worthy end. Recognize that there is an emotion and an action involved because without an action, a value (any value) becomes just an aspiration rather than a way of "being."

Brene Brown[86] is one scientist who has studied courage extensively. Her first research paper is based on the shame resilience theory, which demonstrates that at the heart of many forms of inaction is the shame of feeling unworthy or not belonging to a group that matters to us – whether that is family or work or other kinds of social groups.

---

85   https://www.amazon.com/dp/1592407331
86   https://brenebrown.com/

The Science of Vulnerability

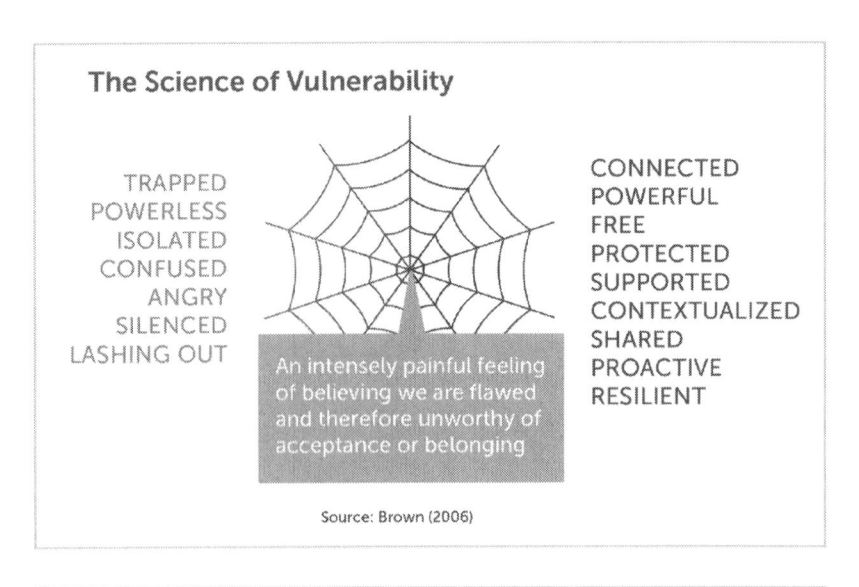

TRAPPED
POWERLESS
ISOLATED
CONFUSED
ANGRY
SILENCED
LASHING OUT

An intensely painful feeling of believing we are flawed and therefore unworthy of acceptance or belonging

CONNECTED
POWERFUL
FREE
PROTECTED
SUPPORTED
CONTEXTUALIZED
SHARED
PROACTIVE
RESILIENT

Source: Brown (2006)

Leading Toward Safety

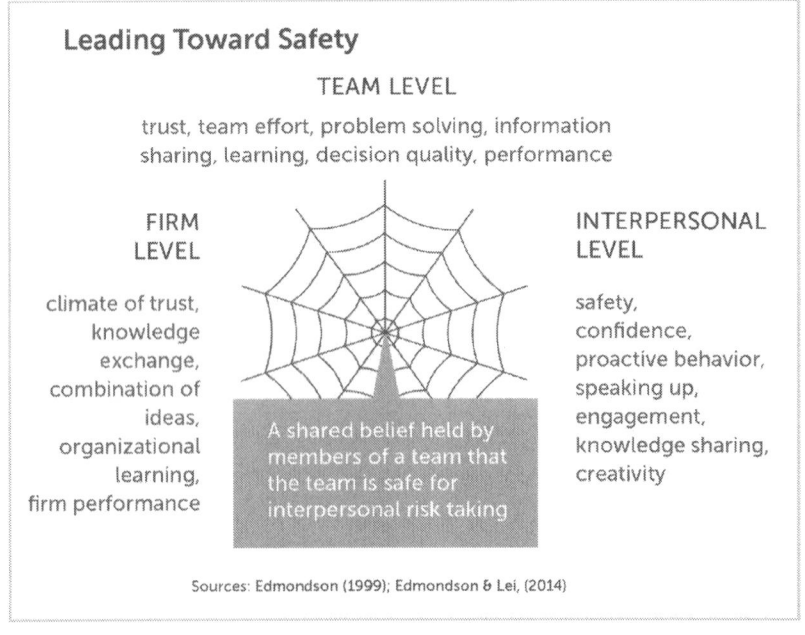

TEAM LEVEL
trust, team effort, problem solving, information sharing, learning, decision quality, performance

FIRM LEVEL
climate of trust, knowledge exchange, combination of ideas, organizational learning, firm performance

A shared belief held by members of a team that the team is safe for interpersonal risk taking

INTERPERSONAL LEVEL
safety, confidence, proactive behavior, speaking up, engagement, knowledge sharing, creativity

Sources: Edmondson (1999); Edmondson & Lei, (2014)

She shows that there is an intense feeling of pain that can get in our way of acting with courage – particularly when we respond to that feeling of shame and unworthiness with a sense of being trapped, alone, and silenced. This is why at times we overstate the fear and impose nobility on those exercising courage.

Courage In The World Of Business

When we study courage in an organizational setting, we find people often feel that there is a risk associated with standing out or even going "against the tide." When they make it clear that they are taking that risk because they believe in something larger, however, their action has a moral standing[87]. In these situations, the act rarely backfires on them. If it seems to at a given moment (imagine an awkward moment in a meeting, where a peer storms out), we find the results often follow in time (i.e. peer coming back to apologize and/or reason).

Nevertheless, it is important to note that there are of course huge myths that get in the way in the workplace. A predominant one is related to being vulnerable in front of others. Vulnerability is often equated to being seen as "weak" by corporate leaders. Some leaders we work with would go as far as to say they are "not that type" – meaning, being vulnerable is not a natural preference for them. This is where it becomes important for us to acknowledge that vulnerability is not a preference, nor is it negative or positive. It is a personality trait available to all and it is neutral in essence. Being vulnerable is hugely beneficial as it opens up space for a dialogue. It serves as a bridge for connection. Of course, inside a collective setting, it may be intimidating for any one of us to propose a new idea or challenge the status quo; yet we can train ourselves to believe any experience is there to provide us with an opportunity to share, to learn, and to grow together.

Being a good leader is a lot about courage because the essence of leadership calls on individuals to take risks. Each one of us is called upon to embrace the discomfort of ambiguity, volatility, and uncertainty; we are expected to lean into the fear of not knowing, of being a source of truth and light, and of being empathetic by allowing space for people to find and cherish their own ways.

Courage In The Fortune 500 Organizations

In our research, we found out that inside certain organizations, where leaders were reportedly acting with courage – meaning they were be-

---

[87] https://uk.sagepub.com/sites/default/files/upm-binaries/39590_Chapter7.pdf

having in concurrence with their purpose and values the majority of the time, they were standing up for their truths, and they were not shying away from offering honest opinion or constructive feedback – employees knew where they stood and which principles to follow. They had clarity around their responsibility areas and put more resources into work that their superiors considered relevant. They also felt comfortable expressing themselves openly and felt better rewarded. As a result, we found that these organizations were more likely to experience a climate of psychological safety as a whole.

Similarly, we identified that inside organizations where leaders were reportedly not exercising courage, employees felt confused about the kind of values and behaviors they were expected to model. On one occasion they might find themselves being rewarded for something, and on another occasion when doing exactly the same thing, they would find themselves being "punished." This created a sense of collective confusion and, as a result, organizations experienced more insecurity as a whole.

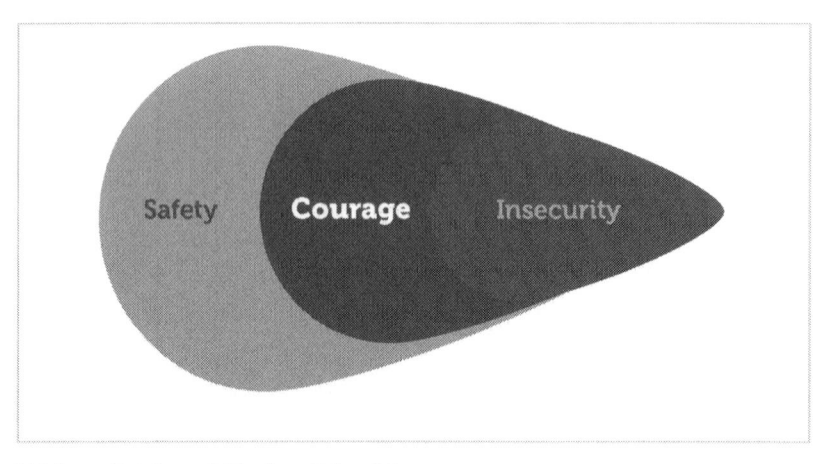

Table 11. Bright and Shadow Side of Courage

At the same time, we discovered that the existence of some of the mindsets previously mentioned went hand in hand with these attributes. For example, cultures that held a mindset of scarcity would often have leaders that failed to show courage. In qualitative interviews, we found that in departmental subcultures with a predominant mindset of scarcity, people operated with the mindset of "zero-sum" and acted as though there was not enough safety, love, acceptance, money or any other resources available. Here, employees felt rather restricted, insecure, and sometimes disengaged from their work. This then meant that people shied away from exercising courage.

Similarly, we found in certain units, there was a culture of perfectionism. There was also by and large a behavior of appraisal by comparison present and the overwhelming sense was that the bar kept being moved higher. This seemed to trigger a sense of shame in people's minds and the majority reported believing that no matter what or how they contributed, they would likely end up receiving some form of criticism. Therefore, they would either develop a feeling of not being good enough, not being capable enough, and at times, not being accepted enough. Needless to say, this sort of "not enough" feeling, when prolonged, reportedly exhausted people's inner drive. It also took away from building trust and a psychologically safe environment – both necessary to demonstrate appropriate levels of vulnerability.

Start By Modeling Courage

Courage embodies a sense of openness. It helps us overcome the fear of intimidation by trusting our life mission (purpose) and values that serve our unique task. When we remain connected to what's true in our heart, the choices we make and/or the actions we take end up feeding into our self-trust and self-respect, helping us move more freely. This connection, in return, feeds our self-esteem and helps us overcome fear.

It is critical then that to be courageous, we first need to lead from within, from our very core spirit, and then act in accordance with our core values, offering a place of unconditional acceptance and love to ourselves and to others. Otherwise, when we are leading from a place of self-protection, we grow self-conscious, which often chips away at our self-esteem and causes a disintegration. As a result, instead of acting authentically and honoring our true wishes, core values or inner motivations, we end up disclaiming our truth and start behaving in ways we think others want to see us. In reality, we are only pushing the responsibility onto others.

Courage is hard and it is okay to not get it right the first time. For example, in the likely event we see a peer getting mistreated by a colleague or some other unfairness at play, and we do not act to stop the behavior, we may find that the feelings of the "victim" are hurt and our inaction has even led them to form a certain opinion about us. More importantly, once we reflect on the particular scenario and evaluate our own behavior, we may find that our self-esteem takes a hit as a response to our inability to act. It is important to realize that implementing policies after the damage is done does not necessarily cure people's feelings, nor shift their state of mind for the future. If we are truly honest about the institutionalization of courage then we must start by modeling it. A positive culture calls upon us to try, to fail, and to rebuild together.

FORESIGHT

Foresight is an act of looking into and thinking about the future. This activity can involve amateur or professional, trained or untrained skills, and, because it drives survival through differentiation, it is one of the most critical for sustaining organizational performance and contributing to creating positive environments around us.

Foresight, unfortunately, is at times undermined as it gets labeled as prophecy, but it is neither prophecy, nor prediction. Foresight does not aim to predict the future – to unveil it as if it were predetermined – rather, it helps us build it. It invites us to consider the future as something that we can create and/or shape, rather than as something already decided.

From a scientific point of view, there are two elements to foresight[88]:

> 1. A mental and sensory representation of things that are not yet present or a sense or feeling of what may be or what may come, and,

---

88   https://www.sciencedirect.com/science/article/abs/pii/S0016328715001159

2. A memory that connects the past to what we know about the future.

When we become able to gear our attention to the experience in the present, not always and frantically looking for evidence to rationalize, we become better connected to a higher sense of vision and creative forces. This is why we often refer to foresight as "reality-based consciousness." Those times when we can surrender to the simplicity of "being" and grow highly attentive of the space, the people, the surroundings around us, we become more capable of floating in the sincerity and freedom of time and across experiences. This is also precisely why the possibility of practicing foresight feels like voodoo to some people. It feels impossible to focus our attention at that depth and become able and engaged in predicting, creating, and becoming part of realities.

Mindfulness[89] is a critical concept in developing attention. Unfortunately, the term has become cliched to many, but, when we think of the many distractions we willingly engage in, such as having multiple workspaces, multiple computing devices, multiple roles and functions, we start to see its appeal. Once we are able to build a basic and honest competency of presence and discover its life-giving energy, we are introduced to a whole new way of life, and with practice, new insights and opportunities present themselves to us.

Foresight In The World Of Business

As with all of the attributes mentioned, foresight has an immense impact on business outcomes, too. For example, Rohrbeck and Kum[90] developed a model in 2018, looking to understand and assess the "future preparedness" (FP) of a firm. We compared the make-up of FP to the way we define foresight and found the two to be highly correlated. With this formula, Rohrbeck and Kum conducted a mega-study, comparing performance standing data of organizations year on year between 2008 to 2015. They found[91] future-prepared firms

---

89   https://link.springer.com/article/10.1007/s12671-012-0123-4
90   https://www.sciencedirect.com/science/article/pii/S0040162517302287
91   https://www.sciencedirect.com/science/article/pii/S0040162517302287

outperformed their peers by an average of 33% higher profitability, and by 200% in growth. Firms with deficiencies in preparedness faced a performance standing decrease of anywhere from 37% to 108%. In some ways, this should not surprise us because even theoretically, if we consider learning from our relevant past, anticipating the relevant and probable future and experimenting with possibilities to analyze and plan, it is logical to assume we would be better prepared for the future. When we are able to melt the past, the present, and the future and consider a list of scenarios to draw out priorities, we do actually become better informed on the strategy to take.

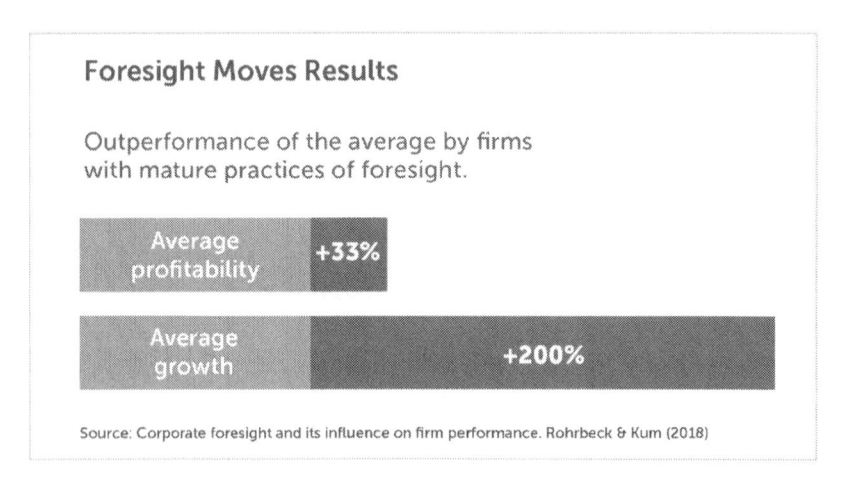

Foresight Moves Results

Outperformance of the average by firms with mature practices of foresight.

Average profitability	+33%
Average growth	+200%

Source: Corporate foresight and its influence on firm performance. Rohrbeck & Kum (2018)

In his book *Thinking, Fast and Slow*, Daniel Kahneman refers to the parts of our brain where he suggests there are two competing kinds of intelligence at play. He specifies one area known as "system 1", an area that relies on speed when it comes to decision making and emotion when perceiving information. System 1 is based largely on our instinct and intuition, when we unconsciously store past experiences that can be rapidly made available to our memories. The second area is affiliated to "system 2", an area where we make slow and deliberate decisions and perceive information more rationally. This area takes in information based on our conscious appraisal of current events and our stored long-term memories which are made available much more slowly[92].

---

92   https://www.amazon.com/Thinking-Fast-Slow-Daniel-Kahneman/dp/0374533555

As leaders, today's world is a particularly exciting time to understand how we use system 1 and system 2 in processing information. Throughout history, we have never had the kind of unpredictability of economics nor the pace of socio-cultural change that we experience today. We have never had so many tools and opportunities with which to greatly improve our lives, our organizations, and our world. Yet, at the same time, we never had such a growing number of complex problems such as scaling our manufacturing lines across multiple geographies, competing priorities, and never-ending desires such as more diversified compensation and benefits structures. We rarely experienced the kind of volatility and ambiguity in managing tasks. It is only natural then that we find ourselves struggling to think holistically as we work hard to meet the diversity of demands in our multifaceted roles. Foresight is the core human attribute that can help us in this particular regard.

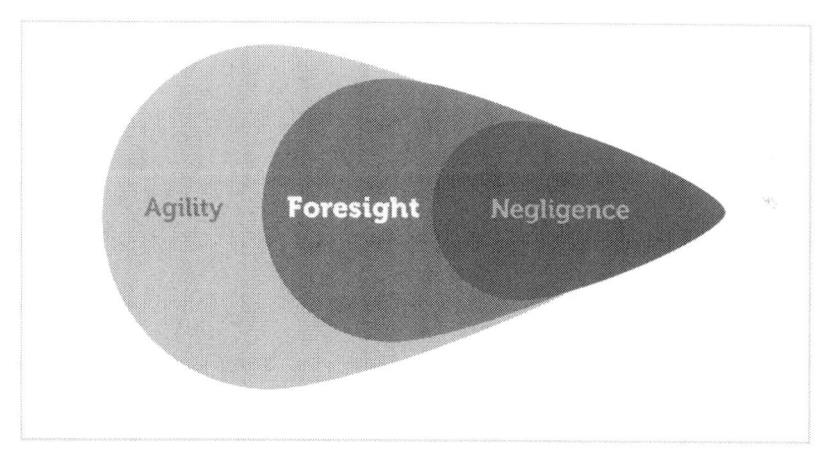

Table 12. Bright and Shadow Side of Foresight

Ever looked at inspiring business leaders and wondered how they are always so in control and actively participating in developing the future? Those business leaders who are recognized as having great foresight actually carve out the time to make a prioritized task list every morning. Then throughout the day, they allow themselves the space to re-prioritize that list several times as conditions evolve.

From a practical, leadership perspective, foresight may be considered as an ability to meta-analyze the past, present, and future. For example, we may see an opportunity ahead. When we explore our memories and discover that we have engaged in such a scenario before, we realize we have previous learnings we can put to use. These recollections can then help us recognize probabilities in the present and weight up today's options consciously, and only from there help us reconsider the possibilities that may lie ahead in the future. Sometimes, we spend way too much time in the past and then we tend to grow blind to the present. When we become unable to sufficiently attend to the present, we tend to overlook what may be an opportunity in the future. This is exactly why foresight requires us to actively relate today's experience to the past and to the future at the same time.

When talking about organizations, foresight often gets mixed up with strategic thinking. To be clear, they are related, but not the same. Foresight is more imaginative and innovative in its essence; it aims to consider a variety of futures at the same time, and is more action oriented. Strategic thinking meanwhile is mostly focused on getting from point A to B and though it may consider some potential ways to do so, it is merely the precursor to strategic execution. Foresight invites participatory ownership[93], and by doing so it creates a collective possibility for building a common future by remaining dynamic as strategic thinking sets out a path to be followed.

Foresight In The Fortune 500 Organizations

During the meta-analysis portion of our research, we were able to validate the impact foresight can have on organizations. Those findings were supported by qualitative data we collected in conversations. For example, when employees reported their leaders to have a firm foot in reality, meaning they were seeing what employees were seeing, leaders were reported to show more presence, demonstrate attentive listening, and exercise appreciative inquiry techniques. Employees felt better supported to employ their intuition when making decisions and organizations, overall, experienced more agility – the nimbleness to move as a whole.

93   https://www.wikiwand.com/en/Participatory_theory

In contrast, in the absence of foresight, we found organizations struggled to experience the same kind of agility. Inside these environments, negligence was prominent and employees reported feeling that they were not connected to today's reality (in a collective sense). They also reported feeling unheard and that everything came as a surprise. Our overwhelming feeling was that inside these environments, it was almost like the concept of change had become a way of life – change for the sake of change – losing its core and strategic value.

Gain Foresight From An Open Heart

It is worth noting that practicing foresight relies heavily on the activation of purpose and courage. As mentioned earlier, the eight attributes are non-linear and are in fact intimately connected to each other. Having developed courage helps vision development because it requires the individual to lean into the unknown, and actively engage in multiple scenario planning. Equally, foresight relies heavily on our ability to hear others well and as they have intended to be heard. This is only possible when we can accept situations for what they are and without an interference of our egos. Such neutrality once again calls on courage because, at times, we may be required to hear things that feel threatening or ambiguous to us. When we exercise courage, we present ourselves by the possibility of weighing options that may have positive or negative connotations, and the catalog of those options is what helps us consider possible future realities and their consequences.

Foresight today may not be a huge science and perhaps it will never fully develop to become one; yet it remains a critical attribute in realizing the future of work and leadership. As globalization continues and the digitalization of platforms, data management, and business processes increase, we will most definitely move from today's generic, data-poor, and ungrounded theoretical and methodological approaches to a more balanced blend of science, empiricism, and art. After all, as Carlo Rovelli, professor of physics and director of the Samy Maroun Research Center for Time, Space and the Quantum[94],

---

94   http://www.spacetimeandquantum.com/

would say "All reality is interaction"; and we are close enough to discover it.

The gateway to exercising foresight may be hidden in keeping an open heart. That is to say that if and when we keep an open heart, accept and care for life around us in all its detail, we may be able to see every instant as it presents itself, without our senses filtering and limiting the way we understand the world around us.

EMOTIONAL INSIGHT

Even if we master our primary core human attributes, and future organizations cultivate thriving environments, where the majority of its employees can unleash and effectively utilize their potential, there remains one major stumbling block – emotion.

Emotional insight[95] is most commonly viewed as the ability to become aware of, identify, express, and work with our emotions effectively. It allows us to see beyond what may be visible to the eye. By paying attention to our complex ways of being and the way we are with others, we allow ourselves the opportunity to explore tucked-away corners of our emotions and discover deeply rooted, buried, and often ignored human needs, feelings, desires, etc. In that respect, you could compare growing emotional insight to igniting the human spirit.

The human spirit, as Sherwin Nuland[96], a professor of surgery and an award-winning author, once wrote "is the result of adaptive biological mechanisms that protect our species, sustain us and serve to perpetuate the existence of humanity." Some of the older wisdom traditions made reference to this state using words such as "*nephesh*" in Judaism, "*nefe*s" in Sufism, and "*phenuma*" in Greek philosophy. Unfortunately, many of us tend to brush off anything related to the human spirit, claiming it intangible. Meanwhile others confuse the human spirit with consciousness; but consciousness is more of an awareness of our

---

95   https://psychologydictionary.org/emotional-insight-1/
96   https://www.wikiwand.com/en/Sherwin_B._Nuland

emotions and responses whereas spirit is more of an enabler for enriching experiences.

Not only do we find that the human spirit is tangible, it is also scientifically measurable[97] in that it affects how we make choices. Viktor Frankl, in his book *Man's Search for Meaning*, writes that "between stimuli and response, there is a space and in that space is our power to choose our response." When we become able to linger in that space, it allows us to discover our free, light-hearted and value-driven ways of being, offering us the possibility of an enhanced, richer experience of who we are and our attitude. The keyword here is again "choice": If we are going to benefit from the human spirit to demonstrate a level of energy to inspire others, we need to be willing to step into the depths of our being, face both the light and dark corners of our emotions, and ride the wave of joy and disparity well. Because only then can we accept our emotions and leverage our insights which will in turn help us meet the emotions of others appropriately. Acknowledgment of diversity of responses to emotions – especially negative emotions – teaches us forbearance. Forbearance helps us understand someone else's emotion at that given time and helps us moderate our responses accordingly. It expands our capacity to comprehend, empathize with, and accept others.

The science[98] of emotional insight points us importantly to the body, calling attention to emotions being physical events and having a distinctive physiology that goes along with tendencies to act in certain ways. Indeed, when we behave in a certain way, we know that a physical experience, such as hearing a loud noise, triggers the energy flow in the body which creates a feeling, like being hot or cold, to ignite a particular early emotion such as excitement or fear. With that physical event, our brain gets involved, and influences emotion formation[99] and decision making.

---

97 http://www.scielo.org.co/scielo.php?script=sci_arttext&pid=S0124-61272013000100003

98 https://www.ncbi.nlm.nih.gov/pmc/articles/PMC2723854/

99 https://www.wikiwand.com/en/Somatic_marker_hypothesis

Similarly, in her book, *Emotional Agility*, a Harvard Medical School psychologist and founder of the Institute of Coaching at McLean Hospital[100], Dr. Susan David shares a scientific approach to expanding emotional capacity. Dr. David argues that the way we perceive our inner selves becomes a key determining factor in how we live and the successes we achieve. For example, maintaining a negative self-image[101] for prolonged periods of time can become destructive to our "being" and may impair our potential for successful relationship building. Maintaining a positive self-image and showing a will to work with our full range of emotions may equip us to develop better navigation (and as a result, happiness) through life. In other words, emotional insight, just like any muscle, can be strengthened and developed by regular practice and through a cycle of reflection. Just like the body, where neglected, our emotions can grow weaker and even perish if left unattended. It is then important to remember that we, as the artists of our own reality, always have a direct influence on the kind of climates we find ourselves in. Our thoughts can serve as a kind of paintbrush, our state of heart as the pallet of our colors, and our eyes as the form of weight coloring in painting our reality. The artist's hand then becomes the vehicle to reflect our spirit in the painted picture.

Emotional Insight In The World Of Business

The majority of us start our adult working lives rooted in dependency. Similar to childhood, we need to gain new knowledge, put things into practice to develop skills, and grow a sense of intuitive intelligence on our way to mastery. The difference is that by the time we reach working age, we have already grown a deep sense of personal identity and a sense of differentiation. The kind of interruptions and mindsets we may have encountered during our early developmental phase(s) and up until we join the workplace, combined with unattainable goals and aggravated expectations mandated by current business environments, end up manifesting themselves as a variety of emotional states:

100   https://instituteofcoaching.org/
101   https://positivepsychology.com/self-esteem/

fragmentation, alienation, emotional touchiness or exhaustion. The effect of these discrepancies between the subjective reality of the individuals and the organization they become part of presents itself as individual behaviors such as low frustration tolerance, diminished self-esteem, loss of ability to manage stress or complexity. These individual behaviors make it significantly more challenging for teams to effectively coordinate, communicate or collaborate, resulting in invisible and unmeasured costs in diminished performances. Consequently, these outcomes often come back and materialize in organizational KPIs such as low job satisfaction scores, low levels of engagement in collective objectives, physical absence from the workplace or a high turnover rate.

Inside an organization, emotions carry extra weight as they heavily shape the habits that make up our cultures' DNA. Habits are often created through repetition and rewards. When we start certain collec-

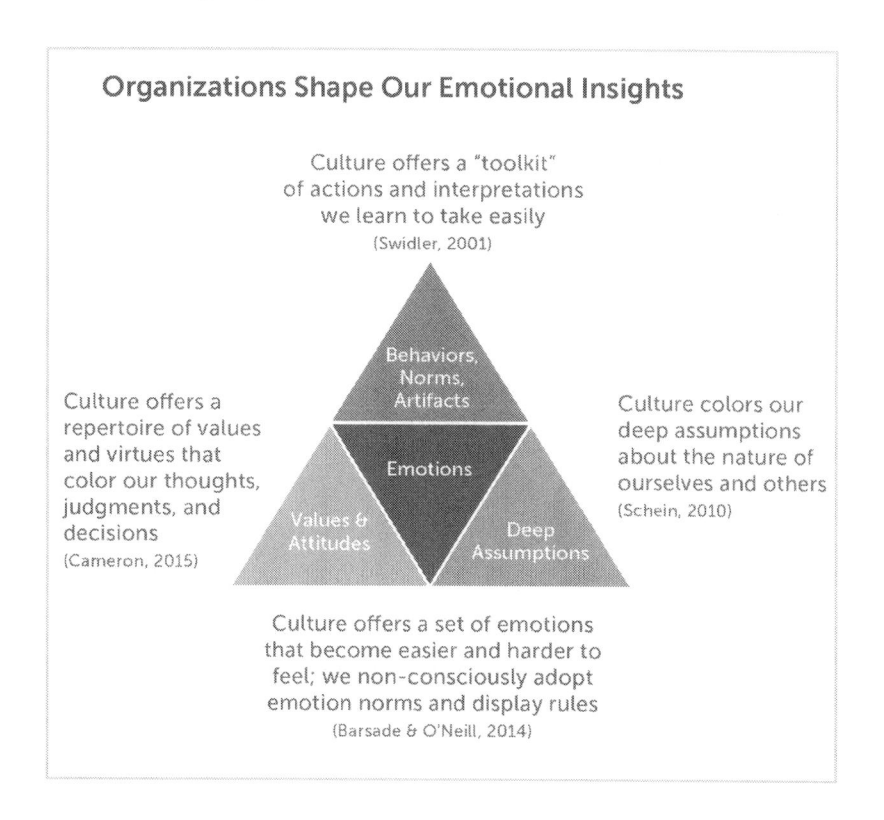

Organizations Shape Our Emotional Insights

Culture offers a "toolkit" of actions and interpretations we learn to take easily
(Swidler, 2001)

Culture offers a repertoire of values and virtues that color our thoughts, judgments, and decisions
(Cameron, 2015)

Behaviors, Norms, Artifacts
Emotions
Values & Attitudes
Deep Assumptions

Culture colors our deep assumptions about the nature of ourselves and others
(Schein, 2010)

Culture offers a set of emotions that become easier and harder to feel; we non-consciously adopt emotion norms and display rules
(Barsade & O'Neill, 2014)

tive routines in an organization without making room to understand what's working and not working for the individuals, we inadvertently end up trapping ourselves in a cycle of stagnation.

The individual insight that comes through emotional awareness and emotional agility can have a positive effect on a whole organization. Therefore, it is a missed opportunity that so often a culture in an organization is only described in values, artifacts, and behaviors, leaving out the biggest driver, emotions. Organizations are living organisms, just like human beings. Organizational cultures give us norms and rules on how to express emotions just as much as they give us norms and rules on how to behave. There is a strong connection between how we feel and how our organization forms its culture, making it almost impossible to theorize about the ideal state of an organization's culture without taking into account the power that emotion has over it.

Emotional Insight In The Fortune 500 Organizations

It has become clear through our analysis that some types of organizational cultures make emotional insight easier, and those that welcome all emotions without labeling them as positive or negative grow inclusive cultures. These are the kinds of cultures in which people embrace the benevolence of the human states and assume the best of each other, supporting a repertoire of virtuous behaviors.

In these environments, we found leaders were reportedly more in tune with their emotions, demonstrated self-esteem, and showed ability to relate in a conscious manner to others' feelings. As a result, employees felt better seen and heard, and organizations did significantly better in employee engagement scores.

Similarly, where leaders were reportedly disconnected from their core emotions and did not have the awareness or capacity to relate to people from a place of understanding, employees felt more shut down and there was more disconnect between the leader and the individual as a result.

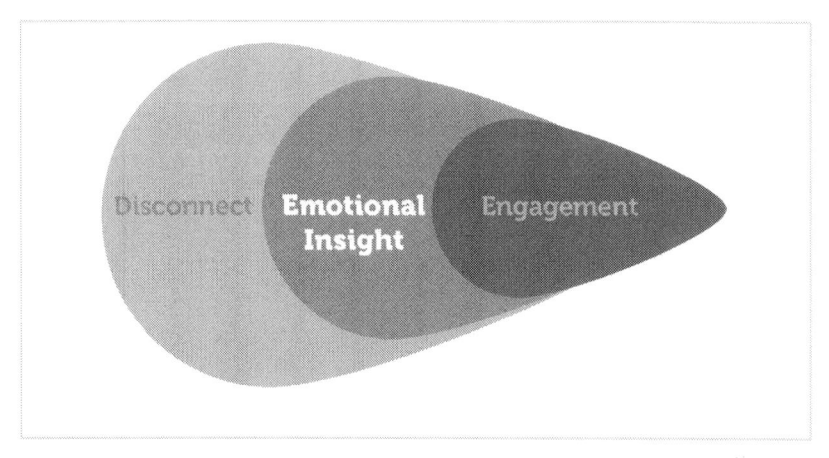

Table 13. Bright and Shadow Side of Emotional Insight

Emotional Insight Over Perfection

Gaining proper emotional insight can be the key to redemption. Our findings present evidence that if we can build self-esteem, self-acceptance, self-respect, self-assertiveness, and self-reliance, we are better at handling our emotions and engaging and connecting with others more effectively.

If "maturity is the ability to live fully and equally in multiple contexts," as the poet and philosopher David Whyte writes, then coming to the understanding that we are not here to control, to judge or even soothe our emotions may be a way of activating and freeing our spirits. The idea is never to be perfect; rather to stand without prejudice in front of our vulnerabilities. The beauty of the entire growth process is hidden in the journey of rediscovery. We can, and arguably should not, aim towards controlling our emotions all the time but to rejoice in our diverse ways of being, both individually and collectively.

WONDER

Wonder is about having a "beginner's mindset." In scientific terms[102], it has three key aspects:

---

102   https://www.wikiwand.com/en/Sense_of_wonder

1. The ability to find, recognize, and take pleasure in the existence of goodness in the physical and social world,

2. An active engagement with and responsiveness to artistic, moral, and natural beauty including the excellence, skills, and talents of others,

3. An active responsiveness through both cognition and emotion, engagement from both mind and heart.

At an individual level, wonder can be best described as an emotion or a state comparable to surprise. It is what we feel when perceiving something new, rare or unexpected, and it is positive. You can think of wonder as "reality-based consciousness" because the more conscious you become, the more wonders you are able to see around you.

We live in a sea of complex and contradictory messages concerning the nature of our value and standards in this day and age. There are constant tensions we are being asked to manage between the agendas of the individual and the collective, the organization and its employees, the government and society, etc. Whether we are a "global senior director of research and innovation" at a multinational corporation or a "veterinarian" in a small local clinic, the majority of us are stretched in our ability to live consciously and beyond our skill development. Even though as human species, our survival, wellbeing and skillful adaptation to a given situation are highly shaped by the quality of our awareness and choices, we have literally become limited in our ability to think, to feel, and to be. This is largely dominated by environmental factors and certainly by some chosen habits.

Our sympathetic systems[103] – the ones that allow us to fight or flight in situations of danger and are meant to serve as a survival mechanism – are now chronically triggered across a large variety of demographics today. The quality of air we take in, the artificial lights we are exposed to, the amount of telecommunications we take part in,

---

103   https://www.health.harvard.edu/staying-healthy/understanding-the-stress-response

the digital vehicles we are required to work with all serve as nonstop stimulators leading to a chronic release of hormones that affect our immune system, inducing stress and inflammation in our bodies. Even if we get seven or eight hours of sleep, go into work on time, and experience what we may consider a productive day managing our tasks and relationships considerably well in the workplace, many of us end up finding ourselves overly exhausted at the end of every single day. This observable shrinkage in capacity has another consequence. In this limited state of "being", the more power we find in our positions, our awarded titles and perceived material successes, the more critical we grow of others' contribution.

This is especially true in today's volume-focused organizational cultures, where questioning is no longer encouraged, and where a shortcut to agreement and to reach a target is the ultimate expectation.

Wonder In The World Of Business

It is a fact that the majority of our work cultures are more concerned with survival of status quo and enforcement of values that support absolute order in reach of a KPI rather than diversity of thought, emotions, experience, and unified pleasure of discovery. As organizational psychologists, we find this predictable path of "unthinking routine" and "I have the answers in me" attitude far more of a threat to business sustainability and to human evolution than any imagined competition. It is our practical experience that where there is no challenge to current ways of being, relating or doing inside an organization, cultures erode faster, leaders miss opportunities, employees fear ramifications, and businesses are often late responding to critical moments of crisis.

In terms of leadership, wonder might seem less apt compared to the other core human attributes, yet, it is a critical part of human evolution and intellectual exploration – especially in relation to the future of work. If you have wonder, you have a sense of curiosity to see and feel the beauty of things around you, like people's talents; and you tend to express more of an appreciation and awe for it. In this way, wonder can help individual leaders overcome the possibility of blind sighting and a range of cognitive bias. By attending to the here and now, we become better aware of options available to us, allowing ourselves the chance to witness what may be present or beyond our imagination and experience.

Once we become able, we discover many benefits of wonder-full living. The first one is expanded awareness into all realms of reality and critical thinking[104]. Trained incapacity can easily lead us to wrong decisions despite the presented reality and most often, when circumstances change around us. This is most relevant for today's business context, where volatility, uncertainty, change, and ambiguity are most prevalent. Awareness, one comes to discover, has no shape or color, and it is beyond presence or absence, coming or going. There is another key benefit to exercising wonder in a collective sense. When we experience a sense of "awe", we physically experience a shrink of ego[105]. When people are measured in this state it is reported that they not only feel happier and their wellbeing gets elevated, but they also

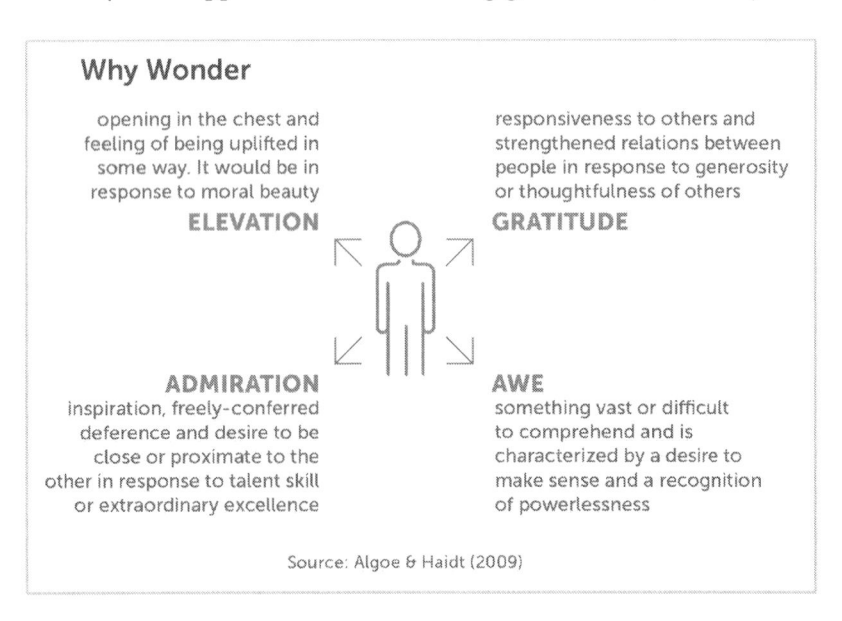

Why Wonder

ELEVATION
opening in the chest and feeling of being uplifted in some way. It would be in response to moral beauty

GRATITUDE
responsiveness to others and strengthened relations between people in response to generosity or thoughtfulness of others

ADMIRATION
inspiration, freely-conferred deference and desire to be close or proximate to the other in response to talent skill or extraordinary excellence

AWE
something vast or difficult to comprehend and is characterized by a desire to make sense and a recognition of powerlessness

Source: Algoe & Haidt (2009)

---

104   https://plato.stanford.edu/entries/decision-capacity/
105   https://www.apa.org/pubs/journals/releases/psp-pspi0000018.pdf

become more invested in a greater good at the same time[106]. As a result, people in this wondrous state of mind approach new realities as a guide to discover alternate truths. In a social setting, this tendency amplifies mutual interest between members to find out about a greater reality together. This behavior, we have come to believe, serves as a practical antidote to innovation.

Wonder In The Fortune 500 Organizations

During our own research, we found that where leaders reportedly showed wonder – for example, they looked to solve complex problems creatively or engaged in appreciative inquiry to understand how something worked – people rated their leaders as being more often active than passive in sharing workload, taking joy in discovering collective intelligence, being more "in the moment" to aid discussions, reaching towards relevant facts and feelings, searching for feedback, engaging in reflection to see and correct mistakes – all in all, better oriented toward continued learning and innovation.

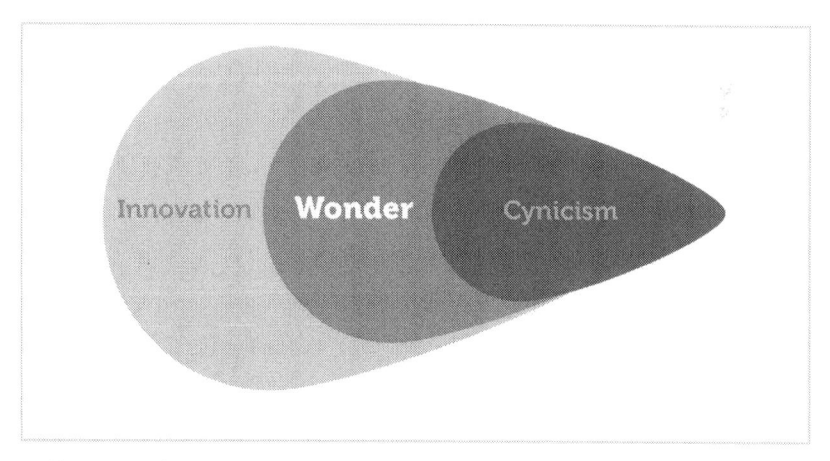

Table 14. Bright and Shadow Side of Wonder

It is also amazing how much impact a lack of wonder can have in an organization. Amongst these organizations, the majority report-

---
106   https://www.apa.org/pubs/journals/releases/psp-pspi0000018.pdf

ed people acting as though they have an answer for everything. For example, it was reported that those in leading positions acted on assumptions, unaware of their individual biases, and teams would engage in misconduct or operate on the basis of procedural biases by, for example, candidate sourcing or compensation reallocation. This sort of overconfidence or "know-it-all" attitude, left to develop over time, led to creativity coming to a full stop.

When during this research we introduced leaders to the concept of "attentive" questions, we found their curiosity grew vastly. Asking questions in general is a uniquely powerful technique that is severely underutilized amongst managers at least. Exploratory questioning that builds our attention around the topic being discussed is a wonderful tool for unlocking value and hidden potential in organizations as it often spurs learning and the flow of ideas exchange.

Overcome Strangeness To Achieve Wonder

When practiced, wonder has immense impact on pro-social behavior[107]. It can enable us to not only notice but also to express more recognition towards someone's work. The challenge, of course, is often to grow our sense of wonder, which requires not only an ability to take in beauty, but also a desire to sift through a feeling of strangeness. This is a particularly difficult state for human beings as we have a natural preference to be in control and have all the answers at the ready.

When we can devote our attention to "now" and show a will to be present in a given moment, we start noticing the growing alternatives inside our minds and hearts. This creates an impulse in us for better cognition[108], taking us from a passive state to actively driving towards information. Showing consistent commitment to presence and trying to consciously approach discussions from different angles without having a need for quick labels (for example, right or wrong) is another helpful way to let our spirits run free.

---

107   https://www.ncbi.nlm.nih.gov/pmc/articles/PMC4114263/
108   https://www.ncbi.nlm.nih.gov/pmc/articles/PMC4635443/

With our growth in emotional insight and on our path to wisdom, wonder can remind us that knowledge has many degrees. One can know by opinion, rely on data or science, and offer insight through intuition. Overconfidence is not only often driven by insufficient consideration of unknown evidence; it can drive poor decision making and hurt trust.

The act of wonder, not only looking for but saving a space for curiosity of one's holistic being, growing the required comfort to sit with attentive and focused awareness and without judgment, may be the way forward.

WISDOM

Melinda Gates wrote in her book *The Moment of Lift*, "Wisdom is not about accumulating more facts; it is about understanding big truths in a deeper way." One can surely recognize a deep truth by the fact that its opposite is also a deep truth. We live in a society that encourages us to think about how to have a great career and leaves us inarticulate about how to cultivate the inner life. The road to success is paved with competition and often that competition is so fierce that it becomes all-consuming for many of us. It is commonly accepted today that information is the key to success but information alone doesn't make someone successful. At its best, information may drive knowledge, yet knowledge alone doesn't lead to righteous action.

In scientific terms[109], being wise refers to having a certain level of awareness and use of intelligence and experience while remaining aware of what is going on around you. There are three key elements to wisdom:

> 1. An awareness of the nested, interconnected nature of the world,
>
> 2. The use of intelligence and experience toward the common good by balancing interests and temporal frames,

---

[109] https://journals.lww.com/hrpjournal/fulltext/2019/05000/The_Emerging_Empirical_Science_of_Wisdom_.1.aspx

3. An understanding of complex, dynamic contexts and working with the dynamics of a system to enable the emergence of more constructive patterns.

That ability to differentiate broadly and in subtle ways the difference between right and wrong, beyond a common understanding, literally offers us a sense of freedom to understand, accept, and trust the reality outside of ourselves.

Unfortunately, this has become a particularly difficult concept to grasp in today's environment, for two reasons: (1) As a society, we have long forgotten about the concept of moral virtue, (2) We tend to overlook the holistic aspects of our being. Instead we think that our mental capacity is sufficient for reaching our limits. There is lost value here because morality as a virtue[110] has served as a necessary means to the development of our collective and organizational structures over the course of history. The idea of vulnerability and struggle in reach of morality is a key cornerstone of our transcendence. When we take, for example, concepts such as failure, mistake or error out of our cultures, it is like we are aiming to work against human nature; and the whole process to individual and collective character building disappears. In other words, we become worthy of respect because of the struggle of our journey to reach moral virtue. Otherwise when we lack the inner constancy, our urge to win the popular vote dominates; we end up turning whichever way the wind blows. We do things that are inconsistent with who we are, diminishing the importance of integrity and losing self-respect. From there, we consciously or unconsciously end up judging people by their abilities, rather than their true worth. In return, when people do not want to be around us, we struggle to understand why.

There is another benefit to wisdom[111] beyond the person-based approach. This is an interactionist or endeavor-based approach, which focuses on wisdom incidents – people's displays of wisdom in real-life

---

110   https://www.jstor.org/stable/3857544?seq=1
111   https://www.researchgate.net/publication/24182606_Real-Life_Contextual_Manifestations_of_Wisdom

situations. The literature[112] on autobiographical memory and on wisdom suggest that, when wisdom is defined as personal qualities or personality traits, its foundation in autobiographical memory is self-concept. However, when wisdom is defined as actual displays of wisdom, its foundation in autobiographical memory is specific autobiographical memories. In that sense, wisdom triggers intuition and opens the gates of collective memory.

Wisdom In The World Of Business

It is a fact that we have become dependent on data inside our current work environments; however, no matter the credibility, we must acknowledge data is just data. It is a point-in-time reflection of what may be happening. When we push away qualitative exchange (i.e. feelings) in our decision making because we think it goes against rationality, we end up shrinking our ability to see broader patterns. Dismissing the fact that our minds work in conjunction with our bodies means we limit our understanding of the world. For example, organizations that only rely on survey results (i.e. pulse, engagement, etc.) and don't consider anecdotal data to better understand how people are really feeling and/or why might miss some really important insight into how healthy their organization truly is or can be.

Wisdom in the context of leadership refers to the ability to have good, sound judgment[113]. It is a source that sheds light on ourselves and introduces a new appreciation for the world around us. It helps us recognize that others are more than our limiting impressions of them. It fills us with confidence knowing we are connected to nature and those around us. Because of this connection, we are often more resourceful and better capable than we could ever dream of. The people with this quality tend to lead from a place of strong internal cohesion. They have overcome fragmentation to reach a

---

112   https://www.sciencedirect.com/science/article/abs/pii/S0732118X18302095

113   https://www.researchgate.net/publication/235295517_Wisdom_and_now_managerial_wisdom_Do_they_have_a_place_in_management_development_programs

level of integration, which supports the way they are – tranquil, settled, and rooted. These people tend to withstand the hard winds of emotional volatility and they do not easily crumble in the face of adversity. They ground their thoughts, emotions, and behaviors in values that feed their self-efficacy and they understand perfectionism is never an unattainable goal.

As a result of this all-trusting view, wise people try not to prove their worth, but rather to be a guiding light, a moral source of joy to others. They show up consistently and demonstrate dependable behaviors despite the variety of situations around. Wise leaders also understand and act as though everything happens as it should, and they seem to have a growing appreciation for complexities in life. For example, if their team fell slightly short of meeting a specific measure, they look to understand the root cause to lift everyone up rather than getting easily frustrated and pointing the finger. By doing so, they remove the feeling of "labor" and emotional bias from the environment. They accomplish this through their equitable infusion of emotions into the climate and by showing admiration for people's unique skills, by sharing companionship for their effort and by demonstrating gratitude towards everyone's contribution equally.

Finally, wise leaders demonstrate an expanded awareness of the interconnections between things, individual and collective, while keeping a focus of the longer-term horizon in any given system. They understand there is no path to mastery alone and that individual will, reason, and character often are not strong enough to consistently defeat our inner critique and environmental deficiencies. As a result, they invest and act in coordination and in collaboration with others. The coordination is more relational in that it aims to bring the best out of everyone. Collaboration is more about making sure everyone gets to have a role in the play. This balanced focus on depth and breadth contributes and drives the motivation to better inclusion, resulting in organizations experiencing higher and more productive contribution, which in return, builds loyalty and trust.

Wisdom In The Fortune 500 Organizations

In our research, we were able to validate that where leaders were reportedly exercising wisdom – for example, they were able to connect with each individual to bring out their unique talents and ensure there is coherence in the collective in behavior – employees reported feeling better included. We also saw a correlation in the way organizations experienced higher degrees of diversity in thought.

Conversely, where leaders were reportedly not connected to wisdom – either they showed a degree of favoritism or could not drive alignment across team members – employees reported feeling unappreciated, and organizations experienced more ignorance as a result.

These findings are similar to many earlier studies where people play monetary exchange games to either win in the short term by being selfish or win bigger in the longer term by being generous. In these studies, it is reported that the initial decisions that people make about this action – to be generous or not with the group – persists over time and across many people, far beyond the one interaction. When you look closely, you find that the first generous move is still being modeled and enacted again up to six interactions later – and this behavior is copied by many people as well. This is a particularly important finding as knowing we will influence hundreds of others with our "first moves" motivates us to invest in wisdom.

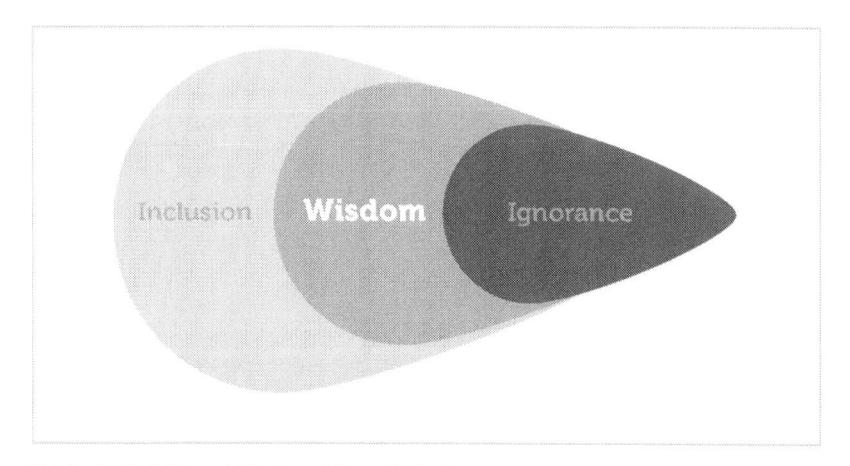

Table 15. Bright and Shadow Side of Wisdom

Moderation, Balance, And Wisdom

Embracing certain ancient virtues such as moderation or balance can help us mature individually or collectively. Unfortunately, these are the kinds of concepts that are often misunderstood and end up working against us in our collective development of wisdom. For example, moderation is often considered a vehicle to finding a midpoint between two parties, and balance an equalizer of scale. In reality, these concepts are engraved in a deep sense of awareness and understanding that there needs to be a relation between the predictor and criteria available. Therefore, it is not only about standing in the middle or finding a common ground, it is about showcasing a desire to discover the potential available in absence of conflict, disconnect, and resistance in the environment. Moderation does not always look to solve arguments; it hopes to achieve a level of consistency, honoring the needs (of parties) for that given moment. It aims for good judgment and insurance of progress rather than an ultimate and immediate solution. Similarly, balance is about honoring everyone's emotions, values, contribution, etc. in reach of sustained harmony and prolonged reach of collective potential.

Finally, leading from a place of trust – growing an understanding of a broader reality that everything will be okay despite us, instead of relying on constant control – may be a path forward. This may be an interesting exercise for many because you quickly discover that control is yet another developed muscle in our bodies. When we use it too frequently, we get tired easily and leverage our resources inefficiently. When we lead from a place of trust, on the other hand, we grow better agency on behalf of ourselves and others. That acceptance of a greater reality gives us confidence (that we will be fine) and a neutral space to guide action. As a result, we show more desire to set up ourselves and others for success and receive more in return without taking away from our internal resources. In the mainstream business culture today, we are consistently told to only provide agency to those who are "deserving." The impact of this is that people are not able to receive love because it feels unearned or not equally distributed.

It is an interesting phenomenon we find ourselves in. Despite being the most developed species, we are not quite developed well enough to comprehend reality in its honest complexity. We are often divided in the core way of our being – perhaps because of our governing structures (i.e. education systems); but we certainly become part of the will that naturally pulls us back because our egos are constantly rewarded for their skewed behavior. We can choose to stand by and not within the meritocratic systems that encourage narrowing. We have a way of questioning traditions (why we do something in the first place), and we have a choice in how we develop – whether through failing, learning, sweating, laughing, and teaching. As a wise man once said: "The heart cannot be taught in a classroom intellectually... Good, wise hearts are obtained through lifetimes of diligent effort to dig deeply within and heal lifetime scars..."

COMPASSION

When we think of compassion, we often visualize a grandiose act; however, when we think back on our experiences, it is actually the little things – the day to day – that we end up remembering.

Compassion is about recognizing someone's suffering and acting to eliminate it at large. When we exercise compassion, we take on someone else's thoughts and feelings, engage in experience sharing, showing empathic concern, and act to remove suffering. In that sense, compassion is more than a feeling, it is a process that has to be learned. There are the steps of recognizing the pain, interpreting the pain, holding space for one's emotional state, and taking an action to remove or alleviate the pain.

Compassion, in scientific terms, has three elements[114]:

1. A sensitivity to the pain or suffering of another, coupled with the deep desire to alleviate that suffering,

---

114   https://www.oxfordhandbooks.com/view/10.1093/oxfordhb/9780190464684.001.0001/oxfordhb-9780190464684

2. Beyond motivation, an active pursuit of alleviating distress for others and in systems,

3. The ability to coordinate and catalyze action across many to respond to suffering.

One of the most common assumptions is that compassion is the same as empathic care. Though the two are related, it is important to delineate the differences between sympathy, empathy, and compassion. Let's think about an example: Imagine seeing someone fall over in the street. Being sympathetic, you may walk by and say "Oh, I see you fell over, I am sorry, that must hurt!" Following that remark, you would simply walk away. Being empathic, you may say "Oh, I see you fell over! I have been there, it hurts but hold on, help is coming!" Following that remark, you may wait a few moments and then walk away. Being compassionate, you may say "Oh, I see you fell over! I am sorry, that must hurt, let me help you up!", and then you may offer the person a hand. Compassion is rooted deeper in our brain systems and because it is action-oriented, actually holds the power to change the way we think, through experience.

Compassion In The World Of Business

It is an unfortunate fact that today's business environment has become so dehumanized and impersonal. Whether we like to admit it or not, there is a lot of seen, unseen, known, unknown pain and suffering in our environments. Gallup State of American Workplace reports[115] that ~25% of the workforce feels like screaming or shouting because of job-related stress; 10% are concerned about an individual at work they fear could become violent. According to NIOSH, 40% of workers reported their job was very or extremely stressful, and that job stress is more strongly associated with health complaints than financial or family problems[116]. WEF Global Gender Gap reports that, at the current rate, the gender pay gap is to close by 2186[117].

---

115   https://www.gallup.com/workplace/238085/state-american-workplace-report-2017.aspx

116   https://www.cdc.gov/niosh/docs/99-101/default.html

117   https://www.weforum.org/reports/the-global-gender-gap-report-2018

As with anything that holds such power, people find incredibly creative ways to avoid and hide from compassion. For example, many executives often say, "I am just not that kind of a leader", meaning a "soft-hearted" one or that they delay or avoid difficult conversations because they "don't want to hurt someone" or "add to someone else's pain." Let us be clear: There is nothing "soft" about compassion. If anything it is significantly harder than leading through aggression, cruelty or avoidance. This is because it requires one to connect to purpose, put effort in, exercise courage, draw on emotional insight, relate to the world with a sense of openness, carrying that deep sense of trust in our hearts. Furthermore, when we look carefully to understand what holds us back from showing compassion, we would likely find it is often an unconscious escape from an opportunity to meet the given conditions with a full heart. At other times, despite knowing what is the right thing to do in our hearts, we may choose not to give someone a hand because our motive to fit in or be liked is greater. The majority of the time, we will later discover what we did to fit in or to be liked – rather than honoring our true self and values – ended up denting our own self-esteem and lost us an opportunity to really connect with someone or the circumstances. Recognizing this kind of dishonoring is what often leads to development of shame or guilt, putting us into a state of trauma effect, causing our heart rate to rise, and preventing us from healthy decision making.

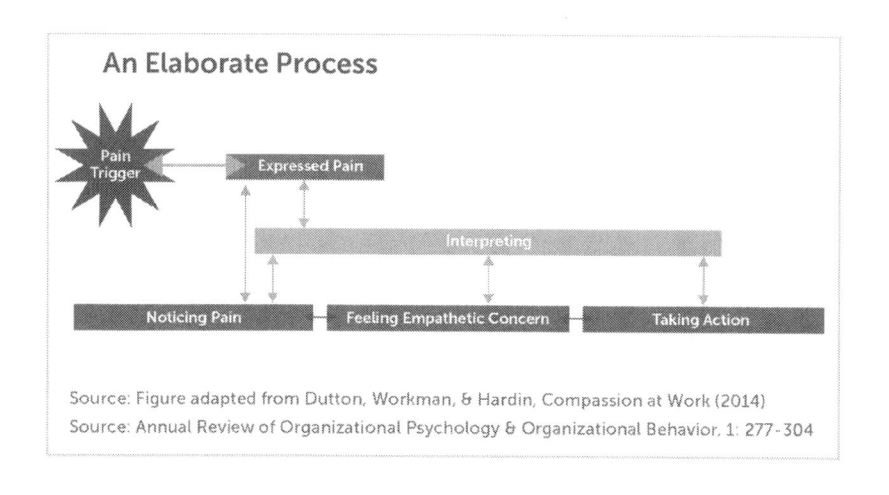

An Elaborate Process

Pain Trigger → Expressed Pain

Noticing Pain → Feeling Empathetic Concern → Taking Action

Interpreting

Source: Figure adapted from Dutton, Workman, & Hardin, Compassion at Work (2014)
Source: Annual Review of Organizational Psychology & Organizational Behavior, 1: 277-304

Compassion In The Fortune 500 Organizations

Where leaders were reportedly acting with compassion – for example, always offering a smile, frequently engaging in active listening, sharing empathic care for everyone's unique situation, etc. – employees felt better cared for and organizations experienced more equity and fairness as a whole.

On the other hand, where leaders were reportedly acting without compassion, employees felt uncared for and organizations experienced indifference as a collective behavior. People we interviewed frequently described this feeling as "growing numbness" to the pain and suffering occurring around because they would report "it didn't matter".

During our qualitative discussions following our research, we heard from a number of employees about the kind of compassionate acts in the workplace that they find make a difference. They mostly referred to appreciation of their unique skills, having understanding relationships with peers and supervisors, active listening and not having pressure from workload.

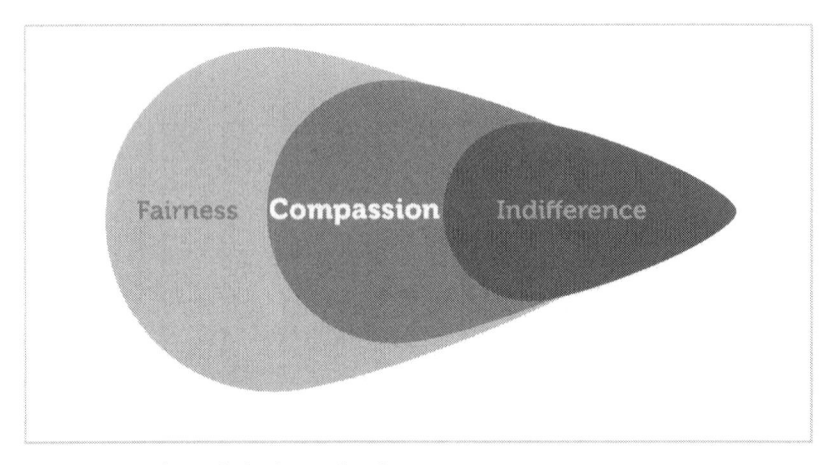

Table 16. Bright and Shadow Side of Compassion

Compassion Means Authentic Connections

Compassion is an instinct for us, human beings. Enabling growth in business requires more than an individual or organizational transformation; it requires an individual and organizational transcendence resulting in authentic connections. For every instinct we pull back from, we need to remember that it is an invitation for someone else's giving in. It is time we face up to the assumptions and myths that are working against our ability to develop compassionate connections. As researcher Brene Brown once wonderfully said, "part of our loneliness is related to our inauthenticity."

Compassionate Presence

Cognitive Reassurance
Discussion of issues
Exploration of possible futures
Explanation of options
Questions and answers to build shared understanding

Emotional Reassurance
Listening actively and reflecting what you hear
Acknowledging the other person's feelings and experiences
Expression of concern and care

Source: Pincus et al., 2013

MASTERY

As our final attribute, mastery is about acting with the trust that any given challenge calls for effort and continuous learning. Mastery also calls upon us to appreciate that the struggle to become, to relate to others or to do work effectively and efficiently is part of the development journey. Mastery requires us to acknowledge that being really good at one thing may not always be sufficient to drive the necessary kind of moral impact or influence[118].

In scientific terms, a masterful "being" has three characteristics[119]:

1. A seeking to increase competence, understanding or skill in ways that promote attainment of challenging and valued goals over the long term,

---

118 https://www.ncbi.nlm.nih.gov/pmc/articles/PMC4434789/
119 https://www.academia.edu/36429661/Motivational_Processes_Affecting_Learning

2. A relishing of challenge and willingness to display ignorance in order to acquire skills, knowledge or experience,

3. An orientation toward growth and development of any capacity over time through focus and sustained effort.

In other words, if knowledge can be considered as the full utilization of information and data related to the potential of one's ideas, intuitions, habits, skills, and commitments, mastery can be considered as the transcendence of and with that information. It is a combination of knowledge, experience, and wisdom; something that is acquired, whereas wisdom is uncovered. The things that you truly know, not facts or statistics, are built by experience with wisdom on top. Mastery embodies an honest sense of enlightenment, offers an invitation for being "one" with the multiple realities, and it suggests we find and cherish joy along the way.

Mastery In The World Of Business

The importance of mastery for organizations has certainly become more of an attention given the current context of knowledge-based economies. It is true that the rapid expansion of knowledge and intensive technologies often results in the increase of market share for an organization; however, there are other significant benefits to gaining mastery inside organizations. When it comes to sustainable growth as an organizational concept, mastery helps build holistic and life-giving experiences.

Though the 17th-century ideology "scientia potentia[120]", commonly referred to as "knowledge is power", materialized in the late 2000s, it would be fair to say that it is only now that we are collectively discovering that knowledge alone is not that sufficient to build mastery. Without doubt, there is a need for a whole range of technical skills and capabilities in order to achieve the strategic business objectives; however, when we consider mastery as limited to technical skills, we miss out a crucial part of leadership.

---

120   https://www.wikiwand.com/en/Scientia_potentia_est

To illustrate this, first imagine yourself as a gardener. The act of gardening requires both an understanding of what each flower and plant needs on a technical level, plus the *consistent and adaptive* practice of this nurturing. This is a generative piece of work and an equally hard one to pursue. As a gardener, we plan, design, plant, seed, water, provide light. But we also struggle. We make mistakes, change the tactics, try different options. All in the name of creating an ecosystem where more of the seeds can become flowers. There is transcendence happening every step of the way between the garden and the gardener. The gardener transfers not only their knowledge and skills; they also form and reform intention depending on the reality one is presented with. Indeed, the best piece of art often forms when the gardener becomes united with the garden. That is the day when the gardener wakes up and realizes the garden has suddenly become a reflection of their labor.

The path to mastery in leadership is almost the same as being a gardener. While you design and work towards reaching a number of outcomes with and through others, the process ends up transforming who you are. A leader plans, divides, delegates work. They also coach, connect, and guide the process of creation and progression. At the same time, a leader is challenged to remain true to themselves and to the vision they intend to drive while developing themselves through their reflection of others. A leader changes shape, color, and quality by day until, one day, they find people are drawn to them without any further effort.

This kind of mastery requires endurance, dedicated time, and continuous effort. It takes hundreds and thousands of repetitions, trials, and errors. In his research, Dr. K. Anders Ericsson[121] says it takes 10,000 hours to develop this sort of expertise. Yet, hours alone are not enough as development of mastery also demands the right kind of focus. A focused mind is a hard one to achieve. Mental focus – psychologically speaking – requires going with the flow, living in the present, and taking mindful breaks for reflection. Being able to say "no", avoiding the myth of multitasking, valuing process, and

---

121 https://www.wikiwand.com/en/K._Anders_Ericsson

measuring results are key. Feedback is the perfect tool for leaders to stay connected and focused as it makes benchmarking a possibility and the necessary adjustments visible to improve for the better. In fact, once a leader realizes the close relationship between having insights and the ability to grow productivity through increased focus, they start to search and surround themselves with more safe and reliable relationships and opportunities. At the level of mastery, there is no need for them to compete with others anymore because they have a better understanding of the dynamics of a system. Instead, they become vested in self-growth and provide inspiration to others. Through our research, we discovered that this is indeed how mastery serves as a tool for rejuvenation inside organizations.

Our promotion philosophies are another important factor pulling back our progression towards mastery. Too often, the organizational systems assume that when a person has been "taught" how to do something well on an individual level, they must be ready to assume responsibility for leading others. This is a false statement. It is true when we start a job, that we first become able to see a single task through to its end and from there, slowly start to perform a family of tasks. As our intuition develops, we often become competent in our jobs and when we are competent, we grow capacity to do more and find space available to help others; but becoming a fully developed contributor to the broader team is not the same as leading others. When we become a solid contributor, others may slowly start seeking our ideas and opinions. This is when we may become able to look across teams/divisions and find opportunities to add differentiated value across teams and individuals. At this critical stage, we have an insight available to us – whether we gain or lose energy by serving others. To develop into a leadership role, we must understand and accept that a coherence must be reached to satisfy our individual energy levels against those of others because mastery requires us to become both lifelong learners and facilitators of others' journeys at the same time. This requires us to acknowledge that organizations only learn when individuals learn and with the right kind of support environment. Individual learning does not guarantee organizational learning but without an individual's love of learning, no organizational learning can occur. At the same time, all learners must be provided the right ecosystem to flourish, first individually then collectively, and that is where the role of a leader comes back in. Of course, it may be tempting to cut the branch that is not blossoming to make the garden look perfect. But this is where most of us fail – we become fixated on the end goal; but mastery lies in knowing the right techniques to use in a given situation and the ability to adjust our way of nurturing as necessary.

If mastery supports sustained growth, you might wonder why we do not care more about mastery. There are a number of reasons why this is. On an individual level, our incapacity for hosting various emotions, and our pull for perfectionism and success tend to get in the way of our ability to adapt and learn. Research[122] has long linked feelings of shame and guilt to perfectionism, which is often demonstrated in behaviors considered as maladaptive. For example, when in a meeting you are asked something you do not have an answer for, a shame-free leader may say "I don't have an answer for this right now; let's find out together." Instead, a shame-prone leader may not say anything or worse, make up an answer and think "I don't have an answer, I am stupid!" There are also a number of reasons on an organizational level that we do not seem to care more about mastery. For example, we do not often understand mastery motivation[123] formation as a psychological force and how it stimulates an individual to attempt and learn independently in a focused and consistent manner.

Carol Dweck's research[124] on mindsets has made this topic very popular – she began studying children and looking at how they responded to challenges in learning. What she found, in a nutshell, is that when oriented toward mastery instead of simply good performance,

---

[122] https://www.researchgate.net/profile/Lawrence_Burns/publication/222899594_Positive_and_Negative_Perfectionism_and_the_ShameGuilt_Distinction_Adaptive_and_Maladaptive_Characteristics/links/59e4a007aca2724cbfe92c32/Positive-and-Negative-Perfectionism-and-the-Shame-Guilt-Distinction-Adaptive-and-Maladaptive-Characteristics.pdf

[123] https://www.tandfonline.com/doi/abs/10.1207/s15566935eed0105_1

[124] https://www.wikiwand.com/en/Carol_Dweck

children relished a challenge and drew value from having to expend effort. But when oriented toward simply performing well, children who faced a challenge and felt they were not performing up to par simply gave up and decided they were not good at learning. In leadership, this orientation toward mastery as the grace of taking on the challenge is a huge part of creativity and handling risks and failures that come with tackling big goals. Mastery makes it possible for us to take joy in the work we must do, even when we think we are really not good at it yet! Similarly, we lack an understanding around the development of brain architecture inside organizations, which provides the foundation for our wellbeing. The architecture of brain construction through hands-on experience is one of the best routes to developing adult learning patterns. As the interaction and experiences shape our ever-developing brains, our cognitive, emotional, social skills as well as the environments we become exposed to, become part of our feedback loops and learning methods.

Mastery In The Fortune 500 Organizations

Where leaders were reportedly exercising mastery, they had become a "true source of light" for their followers. They continuously provided a platform for incremental change through their continued transcendence, and inspired sustained development patterns in others. As a result, on-going learning became part of the culture for these organizations.

On the contrary, inside those organizations where mastery was lacking, mediocracy eventually took over.

Mediocracy can be defined as having only a modest commitment to contemporary values and practices of broader community. It is also shown to have a strong negative impact on productivity and trust. For example, in this study[125], based on a national survey of senior managers in city governments with populations over 50,000, it is reported that in about 41% of cases most managers have only a mediocre commitment to public practices.

125   https://www.jstor.org/stable/3381179?seq=1#page_scan_tab_contents

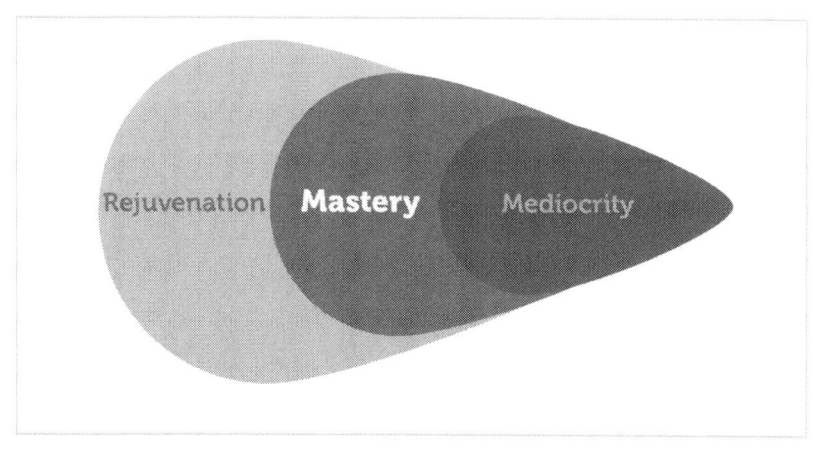

Table 17. Bright and Shadow Side of Mastery

Practice Makes Mastery

We need to understand that organizations learn when individuals develop new habits. Breakthroughs come not through a single attempt, rather through practice. An expert in art, science, music or in fact anything is rarely viewed as an expert because they can deliver a conceptual end; rather because they have a habit of attainment. Take, for example, the Old Masters who would paint not just one masterpiece, but many over an extended period of time. Therefore, mastery requires us to become aware of our guiding creativity and grow trust in our collective ability to overcome hurdles.

■ ■ ■

While these core attributes might seem "known" from their prominence in the most ancient of world traditions, they are being looked at in the new light of scientific discoveries about their power in our becoming and importance in:

1. driving positive relationships,
2. creating effective organizational cultures,
3. driving bottom-line business impact.

Though contemplative and wisdom traditions such as sufis and indigeneous people treat these as values, we also know now that these leadership attributes, when put into practice, have profound effects on the human brain, psychology, and physiology. It is interesting to observe that we seem to have grown a perception that humanity has outgrown these qualities. All of the world's trades – building, farming, producing, designing, teaching – have been invented by human beings. All national borders have been drawn and industries discovered and built by human beings. All civil structures have been modeled, leadership and socio-cultural theories and practices are constructed from within and somehow now, after decades of relying on those inner powers, we seem to have lost our connection to the powers that have carried us forward thus far. This is exactly what makes human beings wondrous creatures. Everything a human being ever seeks for is hidden in one's bodily experiences and yet, the "veils" in front of the eyes and the "clouds" in the mind prevent us from seeing and interpreting deep knowledge available within us. While we become preoccupied with perceptions, assumptions, worldly schemes, and desires, we start to suffer, and over time this suffering turns into pain.

We must realize that we are by and large a product of our experiences and because our individual stories are uniquely felt, they are not always merely factual. We are still analog beings in a highly digital world and very much prone to a lot of human error. Furthermore, all of us bring a shadow and a bright side with us when we are born. The kind of naivety we grow based on our experiences is often a reflection of our own contribution. With every breath, we are presented with an opportunity to integrate parts of us back. It is okay that most of us do not know the difference between what is true to ourselves and what is a perceived status, nor that we understand how to make room to grow the necessary awareness inside. Learning how to lead our unique lives with grace, humility, and love, and to grow a desire to develop with and through our multitudes is the first step to our collective awakening. The kind of true and sustained healing that is going to outlive us and continue for the generations to come requires us to accept our shadow sides along with our bright ones.

We *all* become fearful at times, we shut down, we pull back, we don't want to indulge into new experiences. We frown, we yell, we cry. We all wish to be different at times. The reality is that we are just enough the way we are, and the journey is not about perfection but to become more conscious of who we are. The ability to find our way back to light as often as possible is the necessary step to overcome long-term worry, anxiety, sadness, anger, and fear that shrinks a big part of our abilities.

All these evolutionary states are exactly what we need to meet each other in our humanness. When we can look inside ourselves with clear intention, we find enormous expansion in our minds and bodies, we open our hearts and strengthen our belonging to others. Because you see... Each one of us, every single one of us, is equally worthy of our right to equanimity, dignity, safety, and joy. Together as a community, we can take in humanity, re-introduce hope into our vocabulary and lead a generative part of our human story in business. Together, we can actually evolve our collective work experiences by re-awakening the qualities of purpose, courage, foresight, emotional insight, wonder, wisdom, compassion, and mastery available to us.

In a working environment, we may actually serve each other better by asking what kind of cultures we want to create early on, agreeing on core operating values and principles, identifying operates-mantis to obey behaviors by. This sort of alignment will not only make it a level playing field for everybody, it will also support every-day decision making based on what has been agreed upon.

Because our environments are not "caught up" at the moment to the extent and depth of these attributes, we may need to wear the hats of being a both leader and a follower of our individual and collective transformational journeys for some time to come. Yet, let us remember that it is our self-journeys resulting in individual transcendence that will ignite the transformations of organizations.

PART 4

A BEAUTIFUL WORKPLACE

At 39, following many years of developmental work and corporate work experience, I found myself sitting one afternoon across from my executive coach, who suddenly asked, "Where does it hurt, Sesil?" At first I didn't even comprehend the question to be able to provide a thoughtful answer. "Where do you feel the pain?", she tried again, to which I responded, "I don't feel any pain." She took a gentle breath and asked cautiously, "Do you feel anything?"

Suddenly, I felt a big gulp bubbling up in my throat. I was beginning to sweat and trying very hard to keep my emotions in check. It is most impactful sitting in a space of complete acceptance. It creates conditions non-conducive to hiding so I burst out "It is not me", "it is the child within!"

The child who longed to be free… To run through the green landscape in the freshness of day.

The child who longed to be creative… To play with color and light and discover new realities.

The child who longed to be purposeful… To serve the lives of others, the world, and humanity.

The child who longed to be safe… To be cared for and to be respected no matter the differences.

"What can you influence?" was the question I walked away with and the question that has led to the dream of creating beautiful spaces that allow everyone to thrive.

THE SOUL OF AN ORGANIZATION

When was the last time you walked into a restaurant or a theater, with the sole intention of just watching the staff? How about walking the floors of a factory? Have you ever had the chance to meet workers and shake their hands personally? If you ever get the chance to walk around an organization or sit up close and observe its people very carefully, you would discover a lot of details about how that specific organization operates day by day. If you then do the same over days or weeks, you would come to recognize the behavioral habits that turn the wheel and fuel the operations. And if you observe these behavioral habits for longer still, you would get to know the organization's quality; the quality of its "being", "relating", and "doing." That quality is what we refer to as an organization's soul – or "culture."

A culture often manifests itself onto its new members through their senses. Similar to an air quality inside four walls, a culture carries certain feelings in its transmission. Some organizations will have a version of this culture that is quite light or airy. There will be a gentleness to it that introduces a sense of refreshment. Anyone operating in this kind of culture experiences unexpected fulfillment of joy and typically reports feeling as if they are surrounded by beauty – this was certainly what we collected in anecdotes during our study. When inhabiting this kind of culture, the version offers space and security while at the same time inhabitants find themselves wanting to open up and embrace the quality around them. In that, some cultures make one feel both vulnerable and extremely valuable in one's wholeness. There is another version of this culture that offers purity and triggers a sense of curiosity and wonder. People experience a sudden wish to be playful and often report mentally traveling back to a childhood memory. This kind of culture offers experimentation and its common environments often feature very visual, colorful symbols.

There is yet another version of this culture that is more poignant. This one is rather different in its essence. There is a dryness to it that introduces a sudden sense of irritation. People here experience an unknown feeling of sadness and feel as if they are being watched over. This culture introduces the idea of exposure and sometimes people find themselves growing inflexible and cold by it. There are two key things to remember about organizational culture here: It is impossible to hide an organization's soul, and there are a range of qualities in shape, size, breath, and color.

When it comes to building soul in an organization, we have pretty much got it all wrong. Most of us associate words like "soul" or "spirit" with religion and philosophy, and not with business organizations. But if we look at the origins of these two words, in old Latin[126] they both mean a sense of liveliness across life experiences. Therefore, by definition, they must have a dedicated place inside organizations. It is no surprise then that those organizations that are described as having a high-quality culture (or soul) are often the ones we end up referring to as "thriving" organizations.

A THRIVING ORGANIZATION

A *thriving* organization is one that is well-established and shows sustained levels of performance over a significant period of time. Scientifically speaking[127], there are two conditions to an organization's thriving state. The first is vitality, in which we can measure the individual and collective sense of being alive, passionate, and excited. The second is learning, in which we can measure collective growth that comes from individuals gaining new knowledge and skills. A thriving workforce[128] is not only one where employees mostly feel satisfied and productive, but where they are also engaged in creating the future together, for the sake of the company and themselves. This happens because there is a shared sense of both passion and purpose inside

---

126   https://www.wikiwand.com/en/Spirit
127   http://webuser.bus.umich.edu/spreitze/Pdfs/ThriveinOrg.pdf
128   https://www.ncbi.nlm.nih.gov/pmc/articles/PMC6466057/#:~:text=A%20thriving%20workforce%20can%20be,their%20company%20and%20their%20own.

these organizations. Such high-performing organizations commonly report having a kind of spirituality or soul that sets them apart. For example, these organizations have much better "self-righting" mechanisms built into their organizational architectures compared to their peers. The individual employees often have greater self-esteem than their peers in other organizations, and report mostly operating on the basis of shared trust and collaboration[129]. Many companies we studied, such as General Electrics, Citigroup, and General Mills, we found to have been purposeful about refreshing their practices and policies to safeguard their cultures over the years.

A culture[130] is often defined as "behaviors, values, and artifacts" inside an organization. Many corporations think of culture in terms of their structure, processes, and/or rituals – practices that are agreed or frowned upon. Because of that, the majority of us tend to refer to culture as something separate from us. We see that organizations often use the iceberg model[131]. This is to make the argument that the parts of our cultures that can be seen above the water are just the isolated behaviors and outliers. Meanwhile, it is the submerged part that continues to shape our experiences by and large. Unfortunately, sometimes this visual is misinterpreted as it is both the visible and invisible parts that together form a culture. This interpretation sometimes influences people to think that there are things that are out of their control when a culture is being developed. By the virtue of beliefs, mindsets, and language we consciously or unconsciously set up, we consequently challenge ourselves to comprehend the powerful role of culture in driving successful corporations. Furthermore, by pointing to only outliers, we create mental spheres of separation, otherness, and isolation between groups, and often unconsciously shift the cultural responsibility away from an organization's constituents.

At the other end of the spectrum, it is disheartening that there are still so many companies around the world relying on their cut-throat,

---

129   https://www.ncbi.nlm.nih.gov/books/NBK201683/
130   https://www.wikiwand.com/en/Organizational_culture
131   http://www.ascd.org/ASCD/pdf/journals/ed_lead/el200910_kohm_iceberg.pdf

high-pressure culture to drive their financial success. Especially now that we are learning through a growing body of evidence and science[132] that positive environments have dramatic effects on individual and collective performance. This is very closely related to the way we understand growth inside our corporate cultures. Over the centuries, we have associated the concept of growth most closely with the concept of development, often highlighting the significance of economics. In a number of countries today, an individual is only perceived successful in their professional development if their perceived position (status), title, and/or income can be measured against the hierarchies built and judged by other human beings. And a business is only perceived successful in their organizational development if their perceived position, brand, and/or revenue can be measured against the quota built and judged by other collective groups. This is not to say economics or development is not key to growth. They are. However, growth and development – economic or otherwise – are two independent yet interrelated concepts. Economic development is simply one measure of any potential growth activity.

Let us take an example: The country of China has been reported[133] as the fastest growing country in the past 30 years. Though there may be deniable economic success in China's reported numbers, if we look at their economic modeling, we find out that their model is heavily dependent on exports. To make that model a success, its government often agrees on a number of companies building operations on its own soil, often with no environmental limitations and frequently allowing inequity in terms of conditions for employees or workers. As a result, a company who may be paying its workers in one area a $100,000+ annual salary may easily be permitted to pay their workers in rural China 1$ per day – 1/10th of their peers' salary. The question then is whether it is still appropriate to define this country's reported measures as a "success" given the conditions of its working citizens?

---

132 https://pdfs.semanticscholar.org/65f2/833e478cac47b5cdc8cb2b563e1da45ee08e.pdf

133 https://www.wikiwand.com/en/Economy_of_China

This is certainly not only about China. The majority of economic models we have embedded in our current world order are founded on the promise of "perfect competition[134]", a theoretical market structure in which certain criteria are met. This perfect competition concept has an underlying assumption that people are primarily motivated through self-interest and that they will always have a need for new commodities. These assumptions suggest that where people have an endless need, given the right conditions, there will always be a place for an endless market structure. Recognize that this thought flow takes a skewed view on our core reasons for action. At the same time, the idea of constant competition feeds a set of diminishing mentalities such as scarcity, control, and individualism into our psyches, which, when not properly navigated, introduce a set of detrimental behaviors into our collective way of being.

When we consciously or unconsciously participate in this ideology of continuously and exponentially growing new job families, building new companies, introducing non-binding industry commitments, removing all the obstacles from material production, and presenting the consumer with the promise of a free will to choose, we end up working ourselves towards an endless cycle of consumerism. This view works best to the advantage of economists who often have an implicit expectation for endless, fast, and exponential growth. Interestingly, when we look at comprehensive growth studies[135] beyond economics – that takes into account biology, nature, etc. – we find virtually every outcome of organic growth is not exponential, rather normally distributed, and that sustainable growth always takes time. This makes perfect sense because for any life to make room for growth, it needs to expand in metabolism or in capacity to support development. Growth is a regenerative process that supports on-going development, progression, and transcendence. It is often highly visible, measurable and holistic in its journey. It aims to serve our livelihood and enhance our quality of life, while providing the possi-

---

134   https://stats.oecd.org/glossary/detail.asp?ID=3277
135   https://www.amazon.com/Growth-Microorganisms-Megacities-MIT-Press/dp/0262042835

bility of change by layers. It also needs the right sort of ecosystem to feed itself. One of the very few living creatures recorded[136] as exponentially growing is a cell commonly referred to as cancer.

The definitions behind these core ideologies are essential because a culture is rather embedded[137] in our day-to-day lives and can be encouraged or discouraged. It is important to delineate those formal practices such as structure and roles; organizational stories such as strategies; collective rituals such as celebrations or launches; language and physical arrangements like office or workspace as the *manifestations* of a culture, not the culture itself. It is essential to understand the relationship of collective values and content themes that are espoused from values as well as content themes that are seen to be enacted in individual behavior. Furthermore, it is equally important to understand that cultural manifestations are often interpreted, evaluated, and enacted in a variety of ways by its own members. This is because each one of us has different interests, expectations, experiences, and values. As a result, an organization's culture becomes and serves as the glue holding everything together.

So why does a culture manifest itself differently, you might ask? Because human beings are ever-changing, highly complex organisms, and all organizations go from individual to collective in that organizations too are living organisms and fundamentally human systems. Organizations are highly dynamic in their way of being, complicated in their way of relating, and complex in their mechanics (the way they do their business). While forming, individual human patterns impact the make-up of an organization's collective tissue. Once formed, organizations start to introduce their own behavioral patterns. There is a saying in organizational psychology, that "an organization's capability can be as strong as its weakest link." This is because, beyond individual intersections, interferences, and interfaces, we have a deeply defined sense of interconnectedness and wish to find safety[138] at

---

136 https://www.ncbi.nlm.nih.gov/books/NBK9963/
137 https://hbr.org/2018/01/the-leaders-guide-to-corporate-culture
138 https://library.oapen.org/bitstream/handle/20.500.12657/23080/1007078.pdf?sequence=1&isAllowed=y

an organizational level. As an example, let's say you want to create a peaceful culture inside your organization. You promote "peace" or "harmony" by literally writing it on your walls. But if one of the people within your organization breaks this "peace" rule, either consciously or unconsciously, and with or without your knowledge, you will never get to that end state you aspire to.

SENSE-MAKING

There is another key point about organizations. All organizations provide a common place of purpose and through that purpose an opportunity for "sense-making[139]" for its people. Organizational sense-making involves turning circumstances into a situation that is collectively comprehended and serves as a springboard for individuals to take action. There are often three dimensions to sense-making:

> 1. Direction, which is often referred to as agreement on shared goals
>
> 2. Alignment, which is the organization of work
>
> 3. Commitment, which is the willingness to put aside individual interests for the good of the collective.

Using sense-making in a material way to engage people is a critical responsibility of all organizations. All organizations are tasked to provide a home, a sense of belonging[140] for its people. This is borne out of the definition of people organizing around what they perceive to have in common. When we look at the etymology of several words that define the various kinds of organizations, we see that they refer back to a human's need to connect with those who are alike. The root of the word "corporate", for example, is "corporare" in Latin, meaning "being a part of a group." The root of the word "institution" comes from the Latin "instutio", meaning "coming together for common needs." The root of the word "society" comes

---

139 https://www.researchgate.net/publication/211395920_Organizing_and_the_Process_of_Sensemaking

140 https://www.amazon.com/Belonging-Work-Cultivate-Inclusive-Organization/dp/1732441901

from "societas" which means "being a partner to one another." An organization consists of the patterns of meaning and sense-making as well as connections that link the rise of described manifestations together. That is to say that when we observe a pattern in an organization, we use it to make an interpretation or assumption about the organization. In some organizations, this becomes harmonious through positive patterns[141]. In others, it happens in contradiction or conflict through negative patterns. This is why the culture is commonly referred to as the quality that the form of an organization takes while it self-organizes and grows.

CULTURE FORMATION

When it comes to its formation, a culture inside an organization initially begins as a reflection of its individual human patterns, meaning that the way individuals act and make sense of what is happening around them has an influence on the collective. This is also why organizational culture manifestations include both concrete and abstract content themes. There are collective behaviors, norms, and artifacts as well as there are individual values, attitudes, assumptions, beliefs, and emotions at play inside the given system. Therefore, it is essential to distinguish collective values and content themes adopted by individuals from values and content themes that are enacted in collective behavior. They are highly correlated, yet different entities inside of a culture. If we were to examine culture from a multi-disciplinary perspective[142], we would find that there are four factors at play when as many as just a few organisms come together – initiating the start of a culture[143]. These factors are (1) habit-forming capacity, (2) socialness, (3) intelligence, and (4) language at play that defines the quality of our individual and collective experiences[144].

---

141   https://www.gsb.stanford.edu/faculty-research/working-papers/organizational-culture
142   https://www.uky.edu/~eushe2/Bandura/Bandura1999HP.pdf
143   https://www.ncbi.nlm.nih.gov/books/NBK217810/
144   https://link.springer.com/article/10.1007/s00146-017-0776-6

1. Habit-forming capacity: As previously mentioned, a culture is a system of interrelated and interdependent habit patterns or responses. It does not only depend on individuals; individuals depend on it, too. This is because any habitual behavior, being more susceptible to modification as the result of experience, possesses a certain "survival value". An ordinary habit may die with its possessor (the individual), but once a group has adopted the behavior, the collective pattern of habit will outlive its survivors. In other words, the individual is never a free agent with respect to their culture. This is precisely why we observe at times that inside a "right" culture that provides the 'right' environment, ordinary people do extraordinary things because they start seeing the value and appreciation brought out by the demonstration of certain behaviors. Inside a "wrong" culture, extraordinary people do ordinary and sometimes insatiable things.

2. Socialness: Since culture is not innate, it must first be acquired by each individual and from there, transmitted to others, and then to generations that follow. It must evolve along the way, too. It is this transmission of qualities at an individual level which ensures the continuity of culture in spite of the impermanence of the individual. These qualities have the ability to transport, reproduce, and act as a catalyst for forming "social heritage". In this way, culture is both continuous and cumulative.

3. Intelligence: As a result of this reciprocal relationship we have with culture, it is important to acknowledge that our independence is never really independent in its context. When considering aspirational cultures, it is imperative that we focus on both the attitudes and attributes that are often grounded in particular assumptions and trigger particular emotions, which in time create behavior change for individuals along with artifacts and values. In this way, there is a collective intelligence to an organization's behavior.

4. Language: Though it is at times recognized that language can play a role in the evolution of culture, its power is deeply un-

dermined in terms of transmission and the mechanics of how language can simultaneously encourage both cultural stability and cultural innovation. Language has unprecedented implied influence through presupposition, implicature, and other forms of inference. The way we express ourselves not only marks our identity through variation, it directs our attention and transmits information. When used well, language can bring us together. When not, it can work against us and chain us to realities we may or may not choose to behold.

It is important to recognize that any one of these factors can shift and evolve with multiple dynamics at play and elements supporting the ecosystem. Therefore, when considering readiness and/or planning for a culture or its transformation, we must gain commitment to nurture all factors equally.

BARRIERS TO FORMING HEALTHY CULTURES

One of the biggest challenges organizations face today is that they have let their cultures stray. Though it is absolutely true to claim that any culture has interior and exterior motives as well as visible and invisible behaviors, perhaps a better approach in the future may involve us taking back the ownership through a more holistic and humanistic view. Having a set of values printed and posted on a wall is not the same as aspiring towards a nourishing culture. Such culture is only initiated when we are willing to take responsibility for our individual way of being and from there, care about the collective. This is indeed critical because the essence of an organization's culture is in a perpetual relationship with its people. Put anyone in a toxic culture for too long and they become disjointed from their core values, lose sight of how they make decisions, grow insecurities, avoid conflict, and eventually lose their sense of identity and belonging. Put in a nourishing environment, they become accustomed to gentler ways of being. The key thing to remember is this: a big, catchy slogan that "advertises" your culture may pique people's interest; however, if they do not understand how they can be part of it – how it will change their relationship to their work and others – they will struggle to internalize your jargon or adopted values. Without maintaining an honest sense of ownership at an individual and team level for the collective culture that is being aspired to, resistance, lack of commitment, and disappointment will espouse.

Another very common issue with culture comes from the survival instinct businesses have developed over recent years. The fact is that today's organizations were never designed to evolve proactively and sustainably. They were built for just-in-time discipline and efficiency, often enforced through hierarchy and routinization. Given all the disruption in the ecosystem, a serious mismatch has appeared between the pace of change in the world and the speed at which organizations can respond to it. Unfortunately, the way many organizations are trying to cope with this change is becoming a culture disabler. Many organizations are trying to direct the forces of change and change the change, handle the volume or take shortcuts around the system. This is like driving through a tunnel with no light at the end. As a consequence, employees overwhelmingly feel as though they are constantly rowing against a strong current.

ACCEPTING CHANGE AND VIRTUOUSNESS

A better approach for 21st-century organizations may be to accept change and consider shifting the status quo to provide a platform for transformation instead. This, of course, requires a number of cultural shifts, starting with a fresh look at change. Accepting change would mean we can no longer consider "initiating" change, designing a "change program" or managing change initiatives from "top down". The reality is that what organizations need is not yet another change management program, rather a creation of cultural contexts that first enable inside-out transcendence and then call for organic transformations. This is where the literature for change and culture coincides and the way organizations are thinking about culture becomes equally disabling. There is no outside-in approach to building adaptive, flexible or collaborative structures without the power of learning agility at an individual, team or collective level. This calls for a customized inside-in approach.

If we are serious about creating attractive and thriving cultures, we need to consider virtuousness and bring in a strong character to make this shift happen. Linking virtuous behaviors with organizational behavior is another uncomfortable topic for the business community. Virtuous behaviors[145] are often taught about in relation to morality and ethics whereas organizational behavior is frequently considered in relation to empiricism. This ignorance has been the main reason that critical culture-forming concepts have been largely ignored inside our current organizations. There is no single indicator that can measure multiple elements of virtuousness but there are some key attributes we can discuss. Moral goodness, for example, plays a critical role in developing virtuous behaviors. This is about deciding what may be good, right, and worthy of cultivation for the betterment of the collective at a holistic level. Human impact is another example, which relates to the concepts of self-esteem, control, and resilience. Social betterment is yet another piece of the puzzle that requires a willingness from us to look beyond self-interest and towards the benefit of others. Great organizations are not only about wealth creation. There is also deliberate and mindful corporate and leadership strategy at play, along with other organizational strengths. Virtuousness does not get in the way of profit. Instead it amplifies the impact beyond any figure on a balance sheet.

BEAUTY

Beauty, too, is an unlikely concept in business and at work. Yet, beauty is a quality we want to bring to our future workplace experience. Beauty can appear in many forms: The light of inspiration, the warmth of meaning, the coziness of safety, and the color of joy. Aside from the rooted sense of belonging we need and seek in life, truthfulness and trust is what people expect of organizations, and what is required to build brand loyalty. If we were to regard the world of work

---

[145] https://link.springer.com/referenceworkentry/10.1007%2F978-94-007-6510-8_35

as a piece of art, and critique what we see, we would quickly recognize that it is not very beautiful. Today's common work environments are incredibly metrics-driven – so much so that we see people endlessly arguing over a target missed by half a point.

The environments we become part of are painfully uncomfortable and inhospitable from a psychological perspective. People genuinely struggle to find their way in, express themselves, and feel a sense of belonging. On the whole, today's work environments are also cold and distant from an emotional perspective. In a meeting we may see people smiling but often we are unsure what the other person is thinking or what they will be motivated to do a minute after the meeting is over. Finally, today's work environments are too dark, industrial, inflexible and poorly lit. Ask five people around you and we can almost guarantee you that at least three will tell you they feel like they are working inside a machine.

This picture begs the question of how we actually landed in this situation. How did we become so disconnected from what our bodies are telling us and so distant from our social and affective needs? How did we forget about our day-to-day human necessities? How did we come to devalue balance and the gift of time? Finally, how did we agree that business is no longer here to serve our collective needs and the ecosystem we are a part of? Needless to say, the kind of fragmented, ostentatious, and incoherent experiences our current workplaces offer us is suitable for neither our sustained happiness nor for our sustained wellbeing as human beings. There is a whole body of research emerging around how our surroundings affect our mental, psychological, emotional, and physical health. We now know that people working in green areas sleep better after work, and that spaces with flowers and colorful aesthetics not only create a positive mood, but also positive memories[146]. Beauty can serve as a bridge between what is going on inside and outside of us, and help us move forward with our experiences.

---

146   https://www.ncbi.nlm.nih.gov/pmc/articles/PMC5663018/

LIKE A BEAUTIFUL PIECE OF ART

From beauty we can build intellect and from there, emotional and behavioral practices. Considering beauty can take us out of our typical surface-level thinking and help us discover the why behind our "doing". There are many definitions of beauty. Some refer to it as a reflection of a quiet mind; others see it as a demonstration of continuous energy.

In this context, we call something "beautiful" when it is authentic and simple. There are no pretentious parts to this kind of beauty. An equal appreciation of all one's unique parts is what makes a being interesting. From the way we tick inside to how we behave, beauty ignites for us a sense of freedom and imagination for what is to come. It sparks attention and interest. It invites acceptance for one's holistic experience. There are a number of questions we can ask ourselves about that connection we have come to build between our inner and outer worlds. See if any of the below specifically resonate for you:

- Do you have a sense of what drives you most or what may be your life mission so that you can inspire others?
- Do you have confidence in your own identity to be able to invite and accept the uniqueness of others?
- Are you able to accept your weaknesses to be able to stand with others in times of despair?
- Are you able to offer your innocence to visibly grow and discover others' experiences?
- Do you find any connection between your loneliness and isolation and the spaces of belonging for others?
- How can you better accept your light and shadow sides to find and share joy with others?

Beauty is also encapsulated by transcendence of our collective life as well as our individual livelihood. It creates space for everyone's unique contribution and acknowledges the need to honor and provide for each other. Beauty offers security and reveals preciousness in an organization's members. It offers a tender attitude towards all its stakeholders. Because of this, its basis is in gentleness and forgiving – as a parent or a friend to not intentionally hurt.

Again, there are a number of questions we can ask ourselves about that relationship between ourselves and others:

- What is the best and worst of me?
- How do I come across to others?
- Who do I want next to me during times of crisis?
- When others are in need, am I someone that they would want next to them?
- How can I bring compassion into my relationships as a way to deepen our connection?

Last but not least, beauty is a core moral value for us. Not in the sense of being nice to each other, rather doing right by each other. Beauty honors our humanly necessities and respects our boundaries and capacities. It brings back a lost value of intuitive balance. For me, for example, I tend to want to say "yes" to almost everything that comes my way and so I often risk overwhelming myself quickly. When I remind myself that saying "no" can be beautiful too, because it honors my given boundaries and helps me build better trust with others, I find this liberating. It is similar to the feeling I get when I walk through the middle of a rose garden. It is integral and yet naïve in the sense of purity, like sitting by a tree and watching bees buzz about. It has a quality of tentative labor like being on a high from spending a full day of fun in the sun.

Finally, there are a number of questions we can ask ourselves about the relationship we have with our place in society:

- What are my goals beyond profit making?
- What purpose do I serve in terms of helping humanity flourish?

- How can I best support my team or organization?

- Which common values do I share with people I may not know or even relate to?

- If what we do consequently impacts human lives, what do I want my legacy to be?

From our individual habits – our way of "being" – to our interactions – our way of "relating" – to our intelligence – our way of "doing", our whole work experience is broken. The language we use inside our business organizations is outdated. We need to build stronger characters at every level of our organizations, and they need to have accountability, integrity, and reliance. To transform into agile 21st-century organizations, businesses must grow capabilities while also building a profound legacy of a better version of good.

We know sustainable change is not only internal or external; instead, it requires a delicate balance with high degrees of agility, and starts with continuous inner development of its individuals. Every time any one of us chooses to turn the other cheek when we see examples of indignity, insecurity, and inequality, we contribute to an individual suffering that is reflected on a larger scale. We question if the same would happen to us if we would find ourselves on the receiving end, and as a result our collective memory is scarred. To continue on the same path would be to do the same thing over and over again and somehow expect a different result. The alternative presents an opportunity for unity, of coming together in an act of humanity and rewriting the status quo of business. Whether at a micro or macro level, we can turn pain into joy if we choose to accept the realities facing us.

This is precisely why we have begun the work of visualizing environments free of apathy, allowing people the necessary space and independence to remain connected to their humanities. We want to be able to relate to one another from adult ego-states, meaning we trust in each other's ability to handle truth and make honorable decisions on a day-to-day basis. We want to create workspaces that bring joy, and hold diversity, sensuality, and elements of nature that remind us of our humanities. We want to engage new age leaders in a regenerative process towards re-envisioning the future and building constructive energy towards the making of new work models. We want to embody our collective experiences with:

- Self-acceptance, leading to more holistic human experiences, energy creation, and connection,

- Unconditional and compassionate love, leading to synergy, respectful and empathic co-existence, and better sponsorship,

- Better distribution of power, leading to equity, equality, safety, and co-ownership through greater clarity,

- Practice of white space, leading to successful reflection, calibration, renewal, and increased creativity.

It is not possible to talk about productivity, innovation, and growth in a meaningful way without considering the human aspect. Just as it is not possible to talk about our cognitive abilities, our intelligence, in any meaningful way without factoring in our feelings. There is a strong connection between our minds, our brains, our bodies, and our hearts. That connection defines the way we are (being), how we treat others (relating), and how we approach our work (doing). As businesses and organizations progress on their path towards sustainable growth, we believe not only that a human transformation is possible, but that it will serve as a key differentiator for success.

We are wondrous creatures. Everything we need in life is hidden in our bodily experiences. It is the veils in front of our eyes and the clouds that form in our minds that prevent us from using the deep knowledge we have within us. It may be that we have become preoccupied with perceptions, assumptions, worldly schemes, and desires that raise momentary suffering inside us and it may be that we have lost our sense of joy somewhere along the way towards an unknown destination. It is time we remember the capacities available to us. All of the world's trades – building, farming, producing, designing, teaching – have been invented by us. All of the national borders drawn; industries discovered and built by us. All of the civil structures are modeled, leadership and socio-cultural theories and practices are constructed from within. After decades of relying on those inner powers to build the immense structures we have managed to build thus far, we cannot abandon what makes us most human.

"The sky was lit
by the splendor of the moon

So powerful
I fell to the ground

Your love
has made me sure

I am ready to forsake
this worldly life
and surrender
to the magnificence
of your Being"

*****Rumi*****

Printed in Great Britain
by Amazon